HEARTS *of* COMPASSION, BACKBONES *of* STEEL

Books by Michael L. Brown

Has God Failed You?

Not Afraid of the Antichrist

60 Questions Christians Ask
About Jewish Beliefs and Practices

Answering Jewish Objections to Jesus (vols. 1–4)

HEARTS
of
COMPASSION,
BACKBONES
of
STEEL

HOW TO DISCUSS CONTROVERSIAL TOPICS WITH LOVE AND KINDNESS

MICHAEL L. BROWN

Chosen

a division of Baker Publishing Group
Minneapolis, Minnesota

Published by Chosen Books
Minneapolis, Minnesota
ChosenBooks.com

Chosen Books is a division of
Baker Publishing Group, Grand Rapids, Michigan

Printed in the United States of America

Library of Congress Cataloging-in-Publication Data
Names: Brown, Michael L., 1955- author.
Title: Hearts of compassion, backbones of steel : how to discuss controversial
   topics with love and kindness / Michael L. Brown.
Description: Minneapolis, Minnesota : Chosen Books, a division of Baker
   Publishing Group, [2024] | Includes bibliographical references.
Identifiers: LCCN 2024002213 | ISBN 9780800772475 (paper) | ISBN 9780800773090
   (casebound) | ISBN 9781493447312 (ebook)
Subjects: LCSH: Conflict management—Religious aspects—Christianity. |
   Compassion—Religious aspects—Christianity. | Interpersonal communication—
   Religious aspects—Christianity.
Classification: LCC BV4597.53.C58 B74 2024 | DDC 152.4—dc23/eng/20240506
LC record available at https://lccn.loc.gov/2024002213

Cover design by Peter Gloege

Baker Publishing Group publications use paper produced from sustainable forestry practices and postconsumer waste whenever possible.

24 25 26 27 28 29 30   7 6 5 4 3 2 1

CONTENTS

1. "They Sound Just Like Us" 7

2. Recognize That We All Have Blind Spots 19

3. "Reach Out and Resist" 31

4. Even When Total Honesty Hurts, Love Tells the Truth 45

5. "Overcome Evil with Good" 59

6. Enrolling in Shared Humanity 101 73

7. Hijacked by Demonic Forces 85

8. How to Cope with Rejection for the Gospel 97

9. "The Lord's Servant Must Not Be Quarrelsome" 111

10. Let's Have a Difficult Conversation: *Abortion* 125

11. Let's Have a Difficult Conversation: *LGBTQ+* 145

12. Let's Have a Difficult Conversation: *Race Relations* 171

Conclusion: *An Unstoppable Formula* 187

Helpful Resources 191

Notes 195

ONE

"They Sound Just Like Us"

"They sound just like us." This comment by the pastor of a large and influential church in Texas was as striking as it was surprising, yet it was totally accurate. But whom did he mean by "they" and by "us," and what was the context of his remark? The story I'm about to tell you is the story of the Church in the midst of the culture wars, giving us a perspective on how the Lord would have us live in these volatile and difficult times.

The pastor I just mentioned was almost forty years old, and I had been a mentor in his life since 2014. His congregation had grown dramatically in just four years, and they were active on every front, giving out tens of millions of meals during COVID, rescuing victims of human trafficking, sharing the Gospel with the lost, standing up for the unborn, and creating a vibrant culture of worship and prayer. They were also active politically. They called on elected officials to keep their commitments, stood with candidates who were committed to acting and voting rightly, and even raised up some of their own congregants to run for office.

In 2023, one of those congregants was directly involved in the fight to pass Senate Bill 14 in Texas, a bill designed to protect gender-confused children from receiving life-altering, irreversible surgeries or hormone treatments, procedures that conservatives often refer to as *chemical castration* and *gender mutilation*.[1] But before the bill passed, there was a drawn-out, very intense battle in the Senate, during which the pastor would post daily updates, sometimes calling me and asking for prayer.

This, all of us believed and emphasized, was about the children. This was about saving lives. Emotions were running deep.

After the bill passed, many were thrilled to hear the news. There was great rejoicing, with gratitude to the Lord for His help. This really was about preventing children and young teens from making tragic, life-altering decisions. It was a great win for both parents and kids.

But that was not the end of the story. Shortly after the bill passed, this pastor called and said to me, "I went to the social media pages of those who were fighting against the bill, and *they sounded just like us*. They were saying the exact same things we had been saying: 'This is about the children! This is about saving lives!'"

Our Side, Their Side

What a surprise! They—the political opponents who wanted to harm children, and who had a godless agenda—

sounded as if they actually cared about the children and really wanted to help them. They sounded just like us!

I said to him, "You're exactly right, and it is essential that we understand this. That's how we can minister to them as well."

This pastor had discovered something that many of us have missed in the intensity of the culture wars, something that can be unnerving and disturbing. He realized that many of the people on the other side—those whom we see as our enemies, those who appear to be evil as they push a destructive agenda—are caring human beings too, also fighting for what they believe is right. Some of them are even people of faith.

In *their* eyes, withholding treatments from trans-identified children is criminal, while in *our* eyes, allowing children to receive these treatments is criminal.

Our side says, "These kids have no clue what they're doing at such young ages. If they want to make these decisions as adults, that's up to them. But by all means, we can't let them do this now. How many young women today deeply regret getting full mastectomies at thirteen or fourteen, simply because they were going through a period of confusion? How many young men today can't believe they won't be able to have children because of the hormone blockers they took to stop the onset of puberty? This is about saving the children!"

Their side says, "These kids have been tormented for years, some of them since they were very little. They know they're trapped in the wrong body, and this doesn't just go away. My friend's child has already tried to harm himself, and hardly a day goes by without more young people taking their lives because they can't get the treatments they need and deserve. And the earlier we get them started, the easier their transition will be. Really now, do you want to have the blood of these children on your hands because you withheld the very treatment that could save their lives? This is about saving the children!"

Our side says, "The medical profession is committed to do no harm. Transitioning children is the most harmful thing you can do. It's medical malpractice!"

Their side says, "The medical profession is committed to do no harm. By blocking these doctors from doing their jobs, you are harming the children. It's medical malpractice by default!"

Yes, *they* sound just like *us*.

To be sure, we have valid responses to each and every concern raised by these kids' parents, along with their friends and allies—starting with the fact that the vast majority of kids suffering from gender identity confusion outgrow those feelings after puberty, even if many of them will end up identifying as gay. I stand by "our side" heart and soul, without the slightest hesitation or doubt. We must not participate in the "transitioning" of children.

But what we must grasp here is that most of those on "the other side" are motivated by love, not hate, by genuine (albeit misinformed) concern for the well-being of their son or daughter, not by their adherence to a social agenda. And for every horror story we share with them—including the heartrending stories of the "detransitioners"—they will tell us of someone who found peace after hormone therapy and sex-change surgery (what they call *gender-affirming surgery*). And they would have their tragic suicide stories to share as well.

The questions for us are these: Can we hold firmly to our convictions without demonizing our opponents? Conversely, can we see things through their eyes without weakening our resolve?

Two Core Principles for Effective Apologetics

I have been involved in apologetics—meaning the defense of the Christian faith—almost as long as I have been a believer. That's because I am Jewish, and I grew up not believing in Jesus. And even though my family members were not very observant in their faith, we still went to synagogue on the High Holidays, we still celebrated Hanukkah in the home, I did have a few years of Hebrew school, and I was bar mitzvahed at the age of thirteen. And so, after I came to faith in Jesus at the age of sixteen as a heroin-shooting, LSD-using hippie rock drummer, my father said to me, "Michael, I'm glad that you're off drugs, but we're Jews. We don't believe in Jesus. I want you to talk to the rabbi."

This began my journey of interacting with rabbis and Jewish leaders, a journey that continues to this day, roughly fifty-two years later. But make no mistake about it—I was thrown into deep waters and had to learn to swim the hard way, since I had no one to go to for guidance and I had forgotten the little Hebrew I had learned a few years earlier. Without question, I knew that Jesus was real, since He had dramatically changed my life. But how could I answer these learned rabbis who asked such excellent, probing questions?

Over the decades, I have engaged in many public and private debates and dialogues, not just with rabbis but with Christians from different backgrounds, along with atheists and agnostics, gay activists, Muslims, cult members, and more. The most obvious prerequisite for doing effective apologetics is that we are solid in our faith and understanding. But beyond that, out of all this interaction I have developed my two most foundational principles for effective apologetics:

Principle 1: *Rightly understand what the other person is saying before responding.*

Principle 2: *Feel the weight of the other person's objection.*

The first principle is the easy one: Be sure you *rightly understand what the other person is saying before responding*. The best way to do this is to repeat a person's position back in his or her own words, as in, "So, if I understand you correctly, you are saying this . . . ?" If the person says yes, at least you know you're on the same page. Unfortunately, all too often we speak past each other, because of which we end up passing like ships in the night, without any substantive or fruitful interaction.

The second principle is quite costly: If we are to engage in effective apologetics, we must *feel the weight of the other person's objection*. This is easier said than done! It requires that we do our best to see things through the eyes of our "opponents," getting into their shoes, attempting to grasp the force of their arguments, feeling the weight of their words. Are we really willing to do this? Will we take the time to put on a different pair of glasses? Will we risk the safety of our (often too narrow, hyperdogmatic) world to consider another position?

As I'll explain further in chapter 3, this is something I determined to do when the Lord called me onto the front lines of the culture wars in 2004. I started making appointments with local gay activists to hear their stories, and I started reading everything I could from their perspective. On my end, I was 100 percent sure of what Scripture said about homosexual practice, and I was certain that the "gay agenda" was destructive in many ways. Still, if I was to have God's heart and perspective, I needed to develop sensitivity, compassion, and understanding. After all, grace and truth go hand in hand!

To give you a less controversial example of this second principle, let's say someone comes to you in real distress and says, "I've been struggling with this question for more than twenty years, and it's driving me mad. I've read the Bible through over fifty times, trying to find an answer. I've gone from seminary to seminary and from university to university to speak to the world's greatest biblical scholars and theologians, and none of them can answer my question. I was told that you're a real student of the Word, so now I'm coming to you. Is there any way that you can help me?"

This distraught seeker then shares his or her question with you. You listen, and you reply, "Oh, that's easy! I can give you an answer in less than a minute."

It's pretty obvious that you didn't feel the weight of the person's question. If the answer was so simple and apparent, others would have answered the question long ago, or the person would have discovered the answer on his or her own. You heard the person's words, but you didn't feel their weight. You heard, but you didn't understand.

Going back to the culture wars, I assume that the vast majority of those who read this book will share my pro-life convictions, and that quite likely, you are among them. Abortion is wrong. It is the snuffing out of innocent lives, the slaughter of the unborn within their mothers' wombs. It is evil, and it should not be legal.

Yet have we ever stopped to feel the weight of the "pro-choice" side? Have we considered the agonizing situation of a twelve-year-old girl who was raped by her older brother, only to learn to her shock (and the family's horror) that she is now pregnant? For a score of reasons, wouldn't it be the most humane to terminate the pregnancy as soon as possible? Why expose the girl to shame and the agony of having to carry that child? And what of potential genetic defects? And how will it affect the brother? And who would want to adopt a child born of such a union?

To be sure, situations like that are exceedingly rare, with only 1 percent of all abortions performed because of rape or incest.[2] But do we feel the weight of this? Can we grasp the agony? Can we understand why, in the family's eyes, our position seems cruel and almost inhuman? Even in a less extreme, but also deeply traumatic case of a woman being raped by a stranger, what gives us the right to impose our values on that woman? If her own healing can come through ending the pregnancy, and if it would allow her to move on with her future, shouldn't it be her choice?

Again, I realize that situations like this do not account for the vast majority of abortions, but I use these examples to make a point. There *is* another side to the story, and not all abortions are the result of cavalier choices made by irresponsible people wanting to have sex without consequences.

In the same way, the average gay person is simply trying to live his or her life without hassle or judgment, wanting to work a job and have relationships or care for a family, like anyone else. Put another way, most of those who identify as LGBTQ+ are not activists, are not marching down the streets stripped naked in a "pride" parade, and are certainly not child predators.

Can we do our best to understand these people's positions on the other side, hear their hearts, and feel the weight of their objections, without losing our conviction or resolve? Or is it easier for us to demonize them, pour fuel on the fires of controversy, and keep them at a safe distance?

Seeing the Other Side's Humanity

Right about now, I hear someone saying, "What's with you, Brown? Would you give us the same counsel when it comes to the Nazis? 'Let's do our best to understand why they want to slaughter the Jews!' Is that any different than telling us we need to understand the abortionists and the homosexuals?"

The answer is *absolutely no*, I would not say the same thing about the Nazis, although it's important for us to understand why their message had such appeal to the

Can we do our best
to understand
these people's positions
on the other side,
hear their hearts,
and feel the weight
of their objections,
without losing
our conviction or resolve?

German masses. But the fact is that the lesbian couple who lives next door to you, devoted to raising their two children together (children they had from their previous marriages to men), working hard at their jobs, not using drugs or getting drunk, and really nice neighbors too, are not Nazis. Nor is the single mother of three who is living on a shoestring budget, is in fragile health, was abandoned by her last husband after he impregnated her, and, after weeks of heartrending debate, decided to have an abortion.

Is our own position so weak that we must make others into monsters? Can't we be militantly pro-life while at the same time seeing the humanity of those on the other side? Most pro-choice women are not marching down the streets shouting about their abortions, and plenty of women who have had abortions are hurting on the inside. How wonderful it would be if, in our standing for life, we could reach them too.

It's the same thing with other relevant issues in the culture wars today. If we want to engage effectively, we must do our best to see things through the eyes of those on the other side. And just as it's a good principle that we be able to state our opponents' positions back to them in their own words, it's a good practice to be able to take the other side of a debate as persuasively as possible. If you can do that, that means you've felt the weight of their words and you "get it."

In short, if we want to have God's heart and mind in the culture wars, we need to start here: *We must humanize our opponents rather than demonize our opponents.*

TWO

Recognize That We All Have Blind Spots

The first chapter of Paul's magisterial letter to the Romans describes what happened to the human race as a direct result of our rejection of God. We fell into idolatry, immorality, perversion, and every kind of fleshly sin. That chapter ends with these devastating words:

> Furthermore, just as they did not think it worthwhile to retain the knowledge of God, so God gave them over to a depraved mind, so that they do what ought not to be done. They have become filled with every kind of wickedness, evil, greed and depravity. They are full of envy, murder, strife, deceit and malice. They are gossips, slanderers, God-haters, insolent, arrogant and boastful; they invent ways of doing evil; they disobey their parents; they have no understanding, no fidelity, no love, no mercy. Although they know God's righteous decree that those who do such

things deserve death, they not only continue to do these very things but also approve of those who practice them.

Romans 1:28–32

How wicked people can be. How ugly and cruel. How filthy and despicable. Yes, "they" are really bad!

But that's not all that Paul had to say. Instead, look at his very next words—remembering as you do that in the original letter to the Romans there were no chapter divisions, so there was no break or pause between Romans 1:32 (the last verse of chapter 1) and Romans 2:1 (the first verse of chapter 2):

> You, therefore, have no excuse, you who pass judgment on someone else, for at whatever point you judge another, you are condemning yourself, because you who pass judgment do the same things.

Romans 2:1

So, it isn't just "they" who are guilty; "we" are guilty too! We get angry with drivers who cut us off on the road, honking our horn and glaring at them. They need to pay attention! But when we "accidentally" move into someone else's lane, we're angry with that driver for honking his or her horn at us. *Give me a break!* we think. *I didn't do it intentionally.* How easy it is to justify our own failings while condemning others for those very same failings.

About ten years ago, some of my friends and I were talking with a colleague who was a professional fitness trainer and who offered to run us through some workouts one hour a week. The workouts were intense, and by the end we could barely move. As we were sitting or lying on the ground, he began to talk to us about the importance of healthy eating, reminding us that "abs begin in the kitchen."

I agreed with what he was saying, of course, but then I proceeded to explain that, given my ministry schedule, especially my constant traveling throughout America and abroad, I really couldn't make many changes. Unhealthy eating was a necessary way of life, and no one could really argue with what I said. I made a good case!

A few days later, after working out with another colleague, the same conversation came up. This time, he was the one to explain why, given the intensive ministry schedule he and his wife kept, they really couldn't make the needed changes in their lives to eat more healthily. As he listed his reasons, I said to myself, *Those are the worst excuses I've ever heard. If you want to make changes, you can do it.*

In a flash, I realized my complete hypocrisy. *My* excuses were weighty and compelling and powerful. *His* excuses were weak and wimpy and woeful. I was justified in eating poorly. He was not. What a joke! I silently rebuked myself on the spot.

Merging Boldness with Humility

Yet isn't this what we often do, seeing the faults of others much more easily than we see our own? We can identify the flaws in another person's arguments while perceiving our own arguments as airtight. We can justify (or at the least, explain) the big mistakes we have made while condemning others for much more trivial offenses. That's why Jesus famously said,

> Do not judge, or you too will be judged. For in the same way you judge others, you will be judged, and with the measure you use, it will be measured to you.
>
> Why do you look at the speck of sawdust in your brother's eye and pay no attention to the plank in your own eye? How can you say to your brother, "Let me take the speck out of your eye," when all the time there is a plank in your own eye? You hypocrite, first take the plank out of your own eye, and then you will see clearly to remove the speck from your brother's eye.
>
> Matthew 7:1–5

But notice something carefully here. We *should* help remove the speck from our brother's eye. We *should* make good and sound judgments, as the Lord said in John 7:24: "Stop judging by mere appearances, but instead judge correctly." Paul even wrote, "The person with the Spirit makes judgments about all things, but such a person is not subject to merely human judgments" (1 Corinthians 2:15). Yet Paul also wrote this: "But if we were more discerning with regard to ourselves, we would not come under such judgment" (1 Corinthians 11:31). Here, he was referring to some of the Corinthians who had died and others who were sick because they had partaken of the Lord's Supper in an unworthy manner.

So, yes, we are to make judgments. But we must first judge ourselves, and then we must judge rightly, not judging superficially or by mere outward appearances, not judging hypocritically, and not condemning. And this means that we must recognize our own blind spots. We might be right in the stands we take, but not in the way we take them. We might be right in our positions, but wrong in our personalities. Or we might rightly oppose same-sex "marriage," while failing to address the problem of no-fault divorce in the Church.

This doesn't mean that we retreat from the front lines of the culture wars because of our own weaknesses and failings. But it does mean that we get on our faces first, to repent of our own sins first. It does mean that we do some serious soul-searching, asking God to shine His holy light on our lives. It does mean that we don't simply dismiss the concerns of our critics just because they are on the wrong side of a larger issue. It does mean that we merge boldness with humility, and a clear voice with a listening ear. It does mean that we become aware of our own blind spots.

A Major Lesson from John Newton

Most of us are familiar with the story of John Newton (1725–1807), author of the beloved hymn "Amazing Grace," a hymn that tells the story of his conversion in a very personal way. As he famously wrote, "Amazing grace! How sweet the sound, that saved a wretch like me."[1] Many of us can say, *That speaks of me as well!*

As for Newton, as a young man he served as the captain of several slave ships, buying and selling more than four hundred slaves. As an old man, he was a staunch abolitionist, testifying with vivid clarity about the horrors of the slave trade. What a wretch he had been!

But did you know that Newton had his initial conversion experience while still engaged in the slave-trading business? That he continued to captain a slave ship for more than five years while growing in his faith? And that he initially got out of the monstrous slave trade because of health reasons rather than because of Christian conviction?

Later in life, when fully committed to the abolitionist movement, Newton wrote, "It will always be a subject of humiliating reflection to me, that I was, once, an active instrument, in a business at which my heart now shudders."[2] And he described both the slave trade and his own involvement in it as "abominable."[3]

Yet Newton wrote candidly about the years of his life spent as a slave-trading ship captain, explaining (with my emphasis added),

> Disagreeable I had long found it; but I think I should have quitted it sooner, had I considered it, as I now do, to be unlawful and wrong. *But I never had a scruple upon this head at the time; nor was such a thought once suggested to me, by any friend.* What I did, I did ignorantly; considering it as the line of life which Divine Providence had allotted me, and having no concern, in point of conscience, but to treat the Slaves, while under my care, with as much humanity as a regard to my own safety would admit.[4]

In sum, he wrote, "Custom, example, and interest had blinded my eyes. I did it ignorantly."[5]

Newton, just like us, was a child of his times. Some may protest this, saying, "No way he could be that ignorant! A truly converted man would never accept such a thing, not even for one minute."

To be sure, Newton reflected many years later that during those early years in the Lord, he was not "a believer in the full sense of the word."[6] Yet he certainly thought that he was a believer, and he was definitely walking in the light he had at the time.

And so, my response to you who would condemn Newton comes straight from the words of Paul that I quoted earlier: "You, therefore, have no excuse, you who pass judgment on someone else, for at whatever point you judge another, you are condemning yourself, because you who pass judgment do the same things" (Romans 2:1).

Could it be that we, too, have some serious blind spots when it comes to standing for righteousness? Could it be that we, too, are grossly ignorant in some ways? Could it be that we, too, have failed to stand for certain issues today, issues for which future generations will condemn us?

That, after all, is the very nature of a blind spot. We don't know it's there until someone points it out to us or we discover it for ourselves, often painfully.

Think back to your first lessons driving a car. You thought you had checked the lane next to you, only to hear a blaring horn, or worse still, to come in contact with the car you failed to see, precisely because it was in your blind spot. As I have often said, we don't know what we don't know, and therefore we don't know that we don't know it.

For example, you could be sure that you put all the ingredients into a recipe, because you didn't know other ingredients were required. Or you could be sure that you read all the relevant literature on a subject, because you didn't know there were scores of important books you had entirely overlooked. You didn't know that you didn't know, precisely because you didn't know that you didn't know.

In that same spirit, a Black friend of mine who is a real supporter and colleague once said to me, "Mike, you don't have a racist bone in your body. But there's a lot that you don't know." I took his comments to heart and often start with that presupposition: There's a lot that I don't know.

If you're still wondering how someone could be a true follower of Jesus and yet participate in something as wrong as slavery, even for a time as a new believer, consider what the apostle Paul had to say about his own past:

> I thank Christ Jesus our Lord, who has given me strength, that he considered me trustworthy, appointing me to his service. Even though I was once a blasphemer and a persecutor and a violent man, I was shown mercy because I acted in ignorance and unbelief. The grace of our Lord was poured out on me abundantly, along with the faith and love that are in Christ Jesus.
>
> 1 Timothy 1:12–14

As a zealous, God-fearing Jewish leader, Paul violently persecuted other Jews who followed Jesus, even to the point of their death. Yet God had mercy on him because he did it ignorantly. Once confronted with the truth about Jesus, he repented deeply.

Search Me, God, and Know My Heart . . .

Does this mean that we should never be dogmatic or have deep convictions? Not at all. There are definitely hills that

We do well to walk
in great humility,
recognizing that none of us
know it all or have it all.
And understanding that,
in ways that might surprise us,
we fall short of God's standards
because of our ignorance.

we should die on and truths from which we cannot be moved.

But we do well to walk in great humility, recognizing that none of us know it all or have it all. And understanding that, in ways that might surprise us, we fall short of God's standards because of our ignorance. (And/or because of the spirit of the age in which we live.)

That's why it is essential that we present ourselves before the Lord on a regular basis, examining ourselves by His Word and asking Him to shine the light of His Spirit on our lives. That's why it is crucial that we are teachable and correctable, hating stubbornness and pride like the plague. That's why it is important that we are "quick to listen, slow to speak and slow to become angry" (James[7] 1:19), doing our best to understand where others are coming from before making our final judgments.

When it comes to the contentious cultural issues of the day such as abortion and LGBTQ+ activism, I have no question at all that these are sinful in God's sight. At the same time, I recognize that I could be missing some of the reasons that professing Christians could defend such practices and lifestyles. Not all of them are raging sinners, full of blasphemy and guilt. Some of them sincerely believe that they are standing for what is right and just, and that they are acting in compassion and kindness, out of love for God and people.

Rather than pass these people like ships in the night, we should understand what makes them tick, searching our own hearts for blindness and ignorance as well. For example, when it comes to abortion, is there any truth to the charge that some of us are more concerned with the life of the baby in the womb than with the well-being of the child outside the womb? On other issues, could it be that our views are right but our attitudes are wrong?

This is also why it's healthy to allow your own beliefs and convictions to be challenged. If you are on the right side of truth, with a right spirit as well, you will only be confirmed. If you are wrong in fact or in attitude, you will do well to make the necessary adjustments. We might have more blind spots than we care to admit. (In chapter 12, as we focus on race relations, I'll suggest some ways that we can help identify our own blind spots.)

We would do well to remember the sentiments and prayers of David. He wrote,

> But who can discern their own errors? Forgive my hidden faults. Keep your servant also from willful sins; may they not rule over me. Then I will be blameless, innocent of great transgression.
>
> May these words of my mouth and this meditation of my heart be pleasing in your sight, LORD, my Rock and my Redeemer.
>
> Psalm 19:12–14

David also wrote,

> Search me, God, and know my heart; test me and know my anxious thoughts. See if there is any offensive way in me, and lead me in the way everlasting.
>
> Psalm 139:23–24

Amen and amen!

THREE

"Reach Out and Resist"

It was in the year 2004 that the Lord began to burden me to focus on the dangers of homosexual activism. In the spring of that year, while I was ministering in England, some of my good friends went to a gay pride event in Charlotte, North Carolina, to share the Gospel. We had only been living in the greater Charlotte area since 2003, when our ministry school and many of our core congregational members moved up from Pensacola, and I assumed that we were still in the Bible Belt.

But Charlotte was (and is) a much more "progressive" city, and the gay pride event, which took place in Marshall Park in the heart of Charlotte, absolutely shocked my friends. There were some extremely vulgar, even pornographic, displays right in the presence of little children, and no one seemed to care. In fact, some lesbian policewomen walked hand in hand through the park, and in the end my friends were escorted out of the park by police, even though they had done nothing in violation of the law. It was after that event, after I had heard the reports from my friends and had looked at some of the pictures they had taken, that the Lord began to burden me about what was happening in my new home city, as well as nationwide.

Prior to this, I had not thought a lot about the subject. In fact, it was hardly on my radar. In the first nineteen books I had written, only a few paragraphs even mentioned the subject of homosexuality or gay activism, and in my preaching over the decades, I made scant reference to these subjects at all.

To be sure, I had preached on the dangers of sexual immorality for many years, but always from a heterosexual perspective, warning about the seduction of adultery and the lure of sexual sin. But that was it. Homosexuality was not my concern.

When it came to the moral collapse of our society, I had pointed to some of the most profane elements of gay pride events as evidence of that collapse. And in my full notes to a major message I brought in September 2000, I had written,

> Something is desperately wrong when 50 percent of Americans attend church on a regular basis, yet the best-selling book in our nation's history is a children's book about sorcery and witchcraft. Something is desperately wrong when the Supreme Court can forbid 31 states from outlawing the murder of third-trimester babies. Something is desperately wrong when schoolteachers can legally distribute condoms but not Bibles, when safe-sex classes—paid for by your tax dollars—can teach that homosexuality is

an acceptable lifestyle and that it's okay for consenting fourteen-year-olds to have intercourse—but that same class cannot pray together. We need a revolution!

Gay activism did get a mention, but even here, it was slight. Also in the notes to this full-message text, much of which I left out of the sermon because my notes were way too long (I normally preach without any notes at all), I had written these words:

> This is the hour! If we don't act now, Congress could soon pass bills making it mandatory for religious institutions to hire qualified gays and lesbians, despite their sexual preference. In fact, bills have already been crafted for Congress that would deem the very act of speaking against the homosexual lifestyle hate speech, punishable by law. It used to be considered sinful to practice homosexuality. Today, it's considered sinful to call it sinful! We need a revolution!

All of this was already part of my larger calling to help spark a Gospel-based moral and cultural revolution. But the call in 2004 to help push back the tide of gay activism caught me somewhat by surprise. Why me? After all, my Ph.D. was in Near Eastern Languages and Literatures, not in psychology or counseling or family studies or the like. Plus, I didn't come out of homosexuality myself, whereas in contrast, I had a dramatic testimony of salvation and deliverance from heavy drug use.

Not only so, but I reasoned that there were plenty of others on the front lines already. What could I possibly add? There were men like James Dobson, with Focus on the Family, who had been addressing these issues for years. Or Chuck Colson, who stood as a prophetic voice to the nation. Or Tony Perkins and the Family Research Council, lobbying for righteous legislation and helping educate the Church. Why was I needed too?

Some years earlier, it had made perfect sense to me when the Lord called me to debate learned rabbis and provide apologetics resources, including writing a series of books on *Answering Jewish Objections to Jesus* (amounting to five volumes and more than 1,500 pages total). First, I'm Jewish. Second, I'm a natural debater. Third, I had been interacting with rabbis and Jewish leaders since my earliest days as a new believer. Fourth, I had the necessary academic training. And fifth, no one else was doing it. There was a massive need to be filled, and God called me to help fill it. It was a good and natural fit.

That's why, when people would introduce me as the world's foremost Messianic Jewish apologist, I would jokingly say, "Yes, number one among one!" There wasn't much competition in those early days. I would also say, "It's like playing center on the pygmy basketball team. You don't have to be that tall!" But when it came to pushing back against homosexual activism, there were plenty of good people already doing that, and I was hardly qualified for the task.

Yet I quickly realized that in reality, *no one was going to be able to sit this battle out.* Already in 2004, I also saw that homosexual activism was the principal threat to freedom of speech, conscience, and religion in America. (As I continued to research the subject, I realized that this was not just a matter of concern for Americans. Many other nations were also being affected.) Sooner or later, every believer would be involved in this conflict—in particular, Christian leaders—and all of us would have difficult choices to make.

As evangelical theologian Dr. Al Mohler wrote in 2014, with specific reference to the question of same-sex "marriage" and homosexuality,

> For some time now, it has been increasingly clear that every congregation in this nation will be forced to declare itself openly on this issue. That moment of decision and public declaration will come to every Christian believer, individually. There will be no place to hide, and no place safe from eventual interrogation. The question will be asked, an invitation will be extended, a matter of policy must be decided, and there will be no refuge.[1]

I saw this already in 2004, also recognizing that those gay activists who came out of the closet, in their minds fighting for their very lives, wanted to put people like me in the closet. It was time to push back.

Finding God's Heart for the People

I also realized, however, that this was only part of the story, and if I wanted to have God's heart, I needed to have a real and deep love for those who identified as gay or lesbian or bisexual or queer or trans. A pastoral colleague who is about my age once said that when our generation

35

hears the word *homosexuality*, we think of an issue, but the young generation hears the word and thinks of a person. He was exactly right, and in reality, we are dealing with both people and with issues. Now that the Lord had my attention focused on the issues, I knew I needed His heart for the people.

So I bought as many books as I could to put myself in the shoes of gay and lesbian activists who were fighting for equality. They maintained that they didn't ask to be homosexual any more than I asked to heterosexual, so they wondered why they should be penalized for simply being themselves and for engaging in mutually consensual relationships. As I noted in chapter 1, the vast majority of those who identify as LGBTQ+ are not aggressive activists, let alone sexual predators stalking our children. They simply want to live their lives in peace.

These people were asking questions like, Why did they have to hide their sexuality and their relationships in the closet? Why couldn't they live as everyone else lived? Why was their love less worthy than heterosexual love, especially in the context of long-term relationships with the same partner? And why on earth should their jobs be threatened simply because of what they did in the privacy of their homes and among friends?

I also bought books written by professing gay Christians, with titles like *Holy Homosexuals* by Pastor Mike Piazza, or *Stranger at the Gate* by Dr. Mel White. Dr. White had been a beloved professor at Fuller Theological Seminary, as well as a respected, Bible-teaching pastor, not to mention a ghost writer for Rev. Jerry Falwell. After years of torment, including shock treatments and attempted exorcisms, Dr. White concluded that he had misinterpreted the Scriptures and that God, in fact, had made him gay. Eventually, he founded the organization Soulforce, which states on its website,

> Our co-founder, Mel White, began sowing the seeds of Soulforce after serving evangelical Christians as a pastor, seminary professor, filmmaker, and communications consultant, ghostwriting autobiographies for prominent Religious Right leaders. After publicly coming out as a gay man in 1994, his own autobiography, *Stranger at the Gate: To Be Gay and Christian in America*, received worldwide acclaim; he leveraged his newfound platform to call on likeminded people of faith, asking them to join him in protest of the Religious Right's most prominent figures and their violent treatment of LGBT people.[2]

But I didn't simply read books. I made appointments with local gay activists, some of whom had been quite hostile to people like me in their writings. (By "people like me," I mean conservative Christians who stand for traditional values.) I had meals with them and asked them to tell me their stories, not so I could argue but so I could understand.

All of this—the reading and the interacting—was something I did over a period of years. But the recognition that I needed a heart of compassion for the people had become clear to me already in 2004. Yes, there were issues that needed to be addressed, but there were also people who needed to be reached, and I quickly learned that what we thought was loving and sensitive was not perceived as such by those we were trying to reach.

For example, when we tell a gay-identified person, "We love the sinner but hate the sin," they hear, "You hate me." That's because, in their minds, they do not *do* homosexual things, they *are* homosexual. If you hate their "sin," you hate "them." (Ask yourself for a moment how you would feel if heterosexual practice was considered to be an abomination in God's sight. If you are heterosexual, wouldn't that make you feel as if God personally hated *you* or found *you* to be abominable?)

All of this was growing in my heart through 2004, building to a climax that came on January 17, 2005, at a pro-life event in Washington, D.C., led by my friend Lou Engle. On that day, about 1,000 to 1,500 of us marched for more than two miles down the streets of the city in absolutely frigid weather. As we marched, we had red tape inscribed with the word *LIFE* covering our mouths. The march ended in front of the Supreme Court, where we stopped to pray silently for an extended period of time.

There, in the freezing cold, with nothing else to do but pray and meditate, I received a commission from the Lord as a swirl of thoughts and concepts coalesced into four simple words: "*Reach out and resist*," which meant this:

> *Reach out* to the *people* with compassion; *resist* the *agenda* with courage.

It all made perfect sense! This was the articulation of what had been growing inside me over the previous months as I began to listen and learn and understand. On the one hand, reaching out to those who identified as LGBTQ[3] required tremendous compassion. That's because many of them had been deeply hurt in the past—hurt by the Church, hurt by their families, hurt by their friends. For that reason, they would be extremely sensitive. What seemed like a gentle approach to me might seem harsh and uncaring to them. *Reach out to the people with compassion. All clear, Lord!*

I also knew that resisting the agenda would take a lot of courage. That's because the moment you take a stand against homosexual activism, you will be vilified as a hateful bigot and slandered in the ugliest possible terms. (This had happened to some colleagues of mine, so I was well aware of the consequences of pushing back.) You will not only be called a homophobe and a Nazi, but you will be accused of being a closeted homosexual yourself. You might be pushed out of your job, marginalized in the business world, or rejected as a pastor by your denomination. *Resist the agenda with courage. Once again, all clear, Lord!*

If You're Cut, Bleed Love

From that moment until today, *Reach out and resist* has been the guiding principle in my life and ministry when it comes to LGBTQ+ people and issues, and I can tell you that God Himself has broken my heart for the people. The courage part came more easily to me, since I'm wired by God to be confrontational. The compassion part was the result of the Spirit's work in my life, honoring the efforts I made to understand and to care. (Be assured that the Lord can do the same for you as you yield yourself to Him.)

I vividly recall reading a book in which the author shared painful stories about gays and lesbians who had left the Church and had even become atheists, concluding that the God of the Bible hated them. Why should they believe in a God like that? As I turned the pages—I remember exactly where I was on that particular night—I had to put the book down, falling to my knees in prayer. As I wept, I said to my Father, *God, I don't want to hurt anyone. I just want to help people.* Their pain, in part, had become my pain. This was nothing put on or manufactured. It was—and is—heartfelt. As I have often said, "If you cut us, we should bleed love."

I can illustrate this with a lesson I learned many years earlier, while visiting a pet store on Long Island named "Parrots of the World." My wife, Nancy, and I would sometimes go there with our two daughters, Jen and Megan, checking out the amazing birds on display and occasionally making a purchase (normally buying some of the less expensive, little birds like finches and parakeets). We would always walk over to the section where the large, exotic birds would be perched—macaws and cockatoos and yellow-naped amazons and African greys—and Nancy and I would each pick one, extending our hand to the birds. Immediately, the one I chose would lash out at me with its powerful beak, and I would pull my hand back in fear. But Nancy's bird would immediately perch on her hand.

We would then switch birds, but to my surprise, the same thing would now happen in reverse. The bird that had rejected me would get right onto Nancy's hand, while the one that had accepted her would now reject me. So I asked Nancy, "What's going on?"

She replied, "They can tell that you're afraid."

What a revelation! I came to realize that if a bird could tell that I was afraid (which let it know that it could intimidate me rather than perch on my hand), a person could also tell if I genuinely cared. Saying the right words without having the right heart would not do.

To repeat, then: If people cut us, metaphorically speaking, we should bleed love.

No One Gets to Sit This Out

At the same time, we must be immoveable in our convictions. Put another way, *we need hearts of compassion and backbones of steel.*

Yes, *hearts of compassion and backbones of steel.* This is how we bring grace and truth together. This is how we reflect the heart and mind of the Lord. This is how we represent Him in this world and to this world.

Without a doubt, this can be deeply challenging, and it means living with holy tension. But it can be done, as countless others have learned before us. To say it all once more: *Reach out and resist. Reach out to the people with compassion; resist the agenda with courage.* Does this resonate with you as well?

Perhaps you need more compassion, as I did. Or perhaps you need more courage. Some of this depends on our individual strengths and weaknesses, and some of it depends on our calling.

You might be called to emphasize the compassion side of the equation, giving yourself mainly to outreach (but without compromising your convictions). Or you might be called to emphasize the courage part of the equation,

Hearts of compassion
and backbones of steel.
This is how we bring grace
and truth together.
This is how we reflect the heart
and mind of the Lord.
This is how we represent Him
in this world and to this world.

standing against a destructive agenda (but also walking in love).

Either way, as I realized back in 2004, no one gets to sit this out, whether you're a pastor or a parent, single or married, young or old, in the marketplace or in the home. In one way or another, you will face the agenda or you will interact with a person. So rather than getting dragged into the fray unwillingly, I encourage you to say to the Lord, *Here I am! Send me and use me—and make me fully usable. Give me a heart of compassion and a backbone of steel.*

The Lord will answer this prayer.

FOUR

Even When Total Honesty Hurts, Love Tells the Truth

As a talk radio host, I've received many calls from listeners in pain, but none are so poignant as the calls from mothers who aborted their babies in years past. In some cases, the women break down weeping as they talk about what they did *several decades ago*. In one case, it was a troubled father who called the show, also breaking down in tears as he described how he talked his girlfriend into aborting their child many years back. All the "Shout Your Abortion" campaigns cannot undo the agony of abortion, nor can Planned Parenthood's "lighthearted" Ooti the Uterus emoji campaign.[1]

One caller explained to me that as a staunch feminist she had two abortions, never questioning whether her decision was right. Still, even as a feminist and before she was a follower of Jesus, she would feel pain each year on the dates when her babies would have been born, and this pain began to eat away at her. Only in the Lord was the pain removed.

Many other women have shared their poignant, moving stories as well, yet there was one call that stood out from the rest. It was in September 2017, and it came from a Christian woman who, in a time of financial need as a single mother, took a job at Planned Parenthood. (She called in anonymously.[2]) She wondered if she were doing the right thing, since she wasn't directly involved in performing abortions, and she had Christian friends who told her it was fine for her to work as a receptionist. But she was struggling deep down, also asking me if God could forgive her for what she was doing, and wondering if she might have gone too far from the Lord ever to return.

I asked her, "Can I talk to you with total honesty?"

"Yes," she answered, her voice already beginning to crack.

I said to her, "First, you're not too far gone to go back, but you need to get out of there. You've got no business working there."

Those were my opening words.

You might ask, "Wasn't this a little too blunt? Weren't you being too directive?"

Not at all. This sincere woman called for my advice and perspective. She expressed her inner conflict and concern. And she said I could speak to her with "total honesty."

The hard, difficult truth is that what happens in abortion clinics *is* evil. But that doesn't mean the Lord won't forgive. It's just imperative that we speak the truth in love, and that's what I attempted to do.

And so, as I continued, I emphasized His goodness and love, saying to her,

> But God's merciful and compassionate, and He understands your struggles—a single mom, all the issues we're dealing with. There is forgiveness. Jesus died for any and all sins you've committed, and it's not that you have left God entirely. You just made a wrong decision. It's one that's understandable, but it's absolutely wrong and you need to get out of there and trust God for your next step and He won't fail you. You're not going to end up sleeping on the street somewhere with child or children.

God *is* merciful and incredibly longsuffering. At the same time, it was imperative that she honored Him and did what was right. So I said to her,

> But you absolutely need to get out of there, and, thank God, because you're His child you don't feel right. Because you're His child, you're under conviction. Because you're His child, the joy isn't there and it can't be, because you are facilitating people's abortions.
>
> Whether you're greeting them when they come in, whether you're failing to tell them there are other alternatives, whether you're processing a payment—you're part of that. And it would be, in that respect, no different than say, if you were [alive] during the days of slave trade, that your job was just to register, you know, how many people were on the ship and how many survived or height and weight for sale or something like that. Or if you were in Nazi Germany during the Holocaust and your job was to count the shoes that were taken from the Jewish prisoners

or the gold teeth that were taken or whatever, even if you yourself didn't participate in their death.

So for sure, the Holy Spirit is not letting you be comfortable. For sure, your own conscience is not letting you be comfortable. But don't think for a moment that God's grace is not there. It hurts God as well when relationship is broken with His children. He wants nothing more than to be in active fellowship with you and blessing you.

Just think of if a child of yours—maybe you had a fifteen-year-old [daughter] that made some wrong decisions . . . and because of those [decisions] she now moved in with her boyfriend. And she's thinking, *Boy, if I tell mom I made the wrong decision and I'm so sorry, will she have me back?* She'll have you back with tears. She'll have you back with the biggest hug you've ever gotten in your life.

So yes, I wanted to speak to this dear caller plainly and clearly: *You cannot go back to your job.* But I also wanted to emphasize that there is mercy and forgiveness.

Still, there was more to be said. I wanted her to understand that God is not just merciful; He is also a Redeemer. I went on,

So without question, God will fully restore, and your situation, as embarrassing as it is right now—and I fully honor you calling anonymously; I'm so glad that you called—but God will use this redemptively. You'll be stronger in the pro-life movement because of it. You'll have more sympathy for the people that go in and have abortions, and know the struggles. You will have better understanding of the people behind the scenes performing abortions, or those involved with it. So this can all be redeemed for the good.

But I would immediately give notice—and let me just say this: If you find yourself in financial hardship because of the decision you made—when we're done with this conversation, if you want to just give your name and contact info to our call screener. You won't be put on any list. You won't be put on an email list. This will not be given to anyone.

But we just say, hey, listen, if we know some folks that really help the pro-life movement holistically and that if you ran into some real life crisis, you know, because of this, you can't feed your children the next week or something, we have friends I know that would say, "Hey, we're going to stand with you and in the midst of this. . . ."

Then, with her permission and before praying for her, I asked her this one question: "How long have you worked at the Planned Parenthood place?"

With trembling voice, she told me it had been four months, but that she was always against abortion and that her daughter's middle was name was "Believe" because she had been told she could never have children. But she continued to believe God, and He gave her a daughter. Why, then, did she take the job? Here's what she said:

When I started working there, they told me I wouldn't have to see anything in the back, but that's not really true. As a manager you have to be able to do, you know, all the jobs other than the procedures, because I'm not a clinician. . . . But there is a room in the back and it's called a POC room—Products of Conception. It's where things are processed. [Yes, the remains of aborted babies are called "products of conception," or POC for short.] And you refer to it as either *tissue* or *fetus*, but I saw it for the first time . . . [at this point she began to cry] It's a baby. It's not tissue. It is. It's a baby. There's legs and there's arms and there's eyes and there's babies.

She then explained that when you do ultrasounds during the abortions, if the mother is far enough along in the pregnancy, it looks as if the babies are "fighting back." Then, almost unable to speak, she said, "It's murder. . . . It's just not right."

What a heartbreaking, revealing moment. This was a mother telling the truth about abortion, up close and personal.

As we continued to talk, she told me that even though she was not allowed to do this, she would ask the women who came in for abortions if they had considered adoption. As for Planned Parenthood (and those of like mind), she said they "glorify" abortion as a woman's right. To that argument, she replied that women have the right to say no or to use protection. However, "killing somebody," she said, "is not your right."

So she explained, "I just don't want to go to work Monday."

To which I replied, "No, you can't. There's no possible way you can go to work on Monday."

As I was speaking, she jumped back in and said,

It's not what they tell you it is. It's not what they tell you it is on the news and all the marches that you see. It's not what they say it is. It's what the pro-life people say. They're telling you the truth—it is what they say, how horrible it really is. Coming from inside, I've seen it. It's, it's, it's, it's real bad.

But I just hope to God that if there's somebody listening that wants to have an abortion . . . Don't. Just carry it to term, to adoption. Just don't do that!

All of this was shared with tears and brokenness. When she began to apologize for saying so much, I stopped her and told her that she was saving lives and that we would do our best to shout our conversation out to the world. I then asked her to stay on the line during the break so we could get her contact information in order to help her, before telling her this: "But be sure. No turning back. All right? You know you're being complicit with the murder of children if you go back to this. So make sure—"

She interrupted, "I know!"

Then I continued, ". . . you're out, and that's the reality."

I then asked her about the emotional state of the women after they had their abortions. Was it a happy event for them?

She answered, "Oh, God, no. They cry," often needing the help of "the support people" there with them. She said that they're really somber and that if they have parents with them, "they're very quiet, and they cry a lot."

She then disclosed something I had never heard before. The clinics have journals in the recovery room, where they encourage the women to write down their feelings after the abortion. What did she find written in these journals?

"They're never happy," she explained. "They always regret it."

As I said to the listeners that day, this is the reality, not the picture we get of the "Shout Your Abortion" movement. How tragic.

We continued to talk after the break, discussing whether the clinic pushed people to have abortions in order to make more money and meet quotas. She affirmed that the abortions were "very lucrative." Then finally, before the call was done, I asked her if she believed me when I said that God would fully welcome her back. She assured me that she did, as her pastor had once stated that if you're convicted by the Lord, that's a sign that you are His. That conviction was always there in her life! She knew what she was doing was wrong.

I then strongly encouraged her to get to church on Sunday, and to let Planned Parenthood know right after we got off the phone that she would not be coming in on Monday, and to act responsibly with them in letting them know. I assured her that our pro-life friends would help meet any immediate needs she had. Above all, she needed to confess her sins to the Father, who would fully forgive. I told her that through this call and in the future, she would be saving lives and helping women to have their children. "There're going to be babies born into the world through your story," I told her. "That's how God's going to redeem it."

We then blessed her in prayer, asking God for wholeness for her and her family, and for repentance for the Planned Parenthood workers. To her credit, she called Planned Parenthood that following Monday, saying she would not be coming back, even though, she told us subsequently, they offered her more money and assured her that they were doing good.

There was no turning back for this caller. As she explained in a later written interview,

> Once, I saw tiny fully developed hands in the little Pyrex dish. Tiny, tiny hands perfectly formed . . . that was one of the last straws for me. I kept thinking that one day Jesus will return. I believe in the Rapture. What if He returned and found me doing THIS? I gave up my whole belief system for money. I was paid $70,000 and they offered more when I quit! It was very enticing. [3]

What poignant words! She continued,

> But I just couldn't do it anymore. I used to be really happy, loved life, saw beauty everywhere before I started working there. Then, I started working at Planned Parenthood, and I was always sad, always tired, and really depressed. I even got put on Prozac. A part of me was dying. My husband [whom she married after taking the PP job] used to be a Sergeant in the army, then he got hit by a bomb. He was badly injured and is on partial disability now with the National Guard. But how I felt coming home each day from the abortion center was like a soldier who had come back from war. The emptiness. That's how I felt. Empty. I don't believe we were created to see so much death.
>
> The abortion doesn't end when the baby is removed. It stays with you. You never forget. You never forget and you never get over it. You will always wonder what could have been because that's NOT your only choice. It's wrong. [4]

With the help of the pro-life community, which paid her rent and helped her family with expenses while she interviewed for other jobs, this woman found freedom, hope, and new life. And that same freedom, hope, and new life is available for all women and men who have been involved in abortion. Through the cross, the sin of abortion can be forgiven and the guilt can be removed.

Two Takeaways from the Call

What, then, can we take away from this call? First, outward appearances can be deceiving. Many times, the smile or the celebration on the outside is hiding deep pain on the inside.

Perhaps the reason some women are "shouting" their abortions is because they want to drown out the sound of their conscience? Perhaps the reason that some of those who identify as LGBTQ+ are marching down the streets in "Pride" events is because they are fighting the Spirit's conviction? You never know what the Lord is doing in the lives of the people you meet, especially if they have been raised in a strong Christian home. Those roots are often hard to uproot.

During a chapel service at the Bible school where I taught in the mid-1980s, the Lord spoke to me to go over and minister to one of our students. The Spirit showed me that she was going through a time of deep depression. Immediately, I went to pray for her, looking for her among the other students. But to my surprise, she was worshiping with hands raised and glowing face. *Depression?* I said to myself. *Seriously?*

Yet I couldn't deny the prompting of the Lord, so I shared in this student's ear what I believed the Lord had told me. Instantly, she began to weep, telling me she was under such attack that she had actually contemplated suicide. Outward appearances can be misleading!

Second, love tells the truth. As American economist and cultural commentator Thomas Sowell put it, "When you want to help people, you tell them the truth. When you want to help yourself, you tell them what they want to hear."[5] This is often difficult and uncomfortable, but again, if our focus is on others and not on ourselves, we'll tell them what they need to hear, not what they want to hear.

Proverbs addresses this head on: "Better is open rebuke than hidden love. Wounds from a friend can be trusted, but an enemy multiplies kisses" (Proverbs 27:5–6). And here too: "Whoever rebukes a person will in the end gain favor rather than one who has a flattering tongue" (Proverbs 28:23). This does not mean that we are harsh. Or nasty. Or short-tempered. But it does mean that we refuse to water down the truth in the interest of not making the other person feel bad. Whom, then, are we helping if we water down the truth? Wouldn't that be like a doctor refusing to tell patients that they need immediate surgery, since he or she doesn't want them to "feel bad"?

The whole reason we go to a doctor is to get diagnosed so we can get healthy. "Tell me the truth, Doc, and don't sugarcoat things." That's our sentiment as patients. For doctors, to fail to tell the truth is to commit medical malpractice. Let's not be guilty of spiritual malpractice! As the seventeenth-century minister and Bible commentator Jean Daillé said, "Ministers are not cooks, but physicians

Love tells the truth.
If our focus is on others
and not on ourselves,
we'll tell them what they
need to hear, not what
they want to hear.

and therefore should not study to delight the palate, but to recover the patient."[6] Exactly!

Ministry Requires Clarity

Let's also remember that if we post on social media or respond to a question in a group setting (or, in my case, on a live radio show), others are listening and watching. So while we are careful to speak graciously to those with whom we interact, we must stay faithful to the Lord and His Word, lest we lead others astray. That's why I categorically differed with a well-known minister who once told me, "There are times when ministry preempts clarity." To the contrary, ministry requires clarity.[7]

May all of us learn to speak the truth in love. It will glorify the Lord and save many lives. It will also help us walk in spiritual wholeness and personal integrity, since neither compromise nor harshness is conducive to our well-being in the Lord. In the beautiful picture painted in the psalms, "Love and faithfulness meet together; righteousness and peace kiss each other" (Psalm 85:10). That's what happens when truth is grounded in love and love is grounded in truth.

On November 8, 2018, we received an email with this subject heading at my ministry: "I was the anonymous Planned Parenthood worker who called your show." This was the text of the email:

> I just wanted to tell you, "Thank you" for taking my call that day and praying for me. You would not begin to imagine

where I am now and what all I'm involved with. You were the bridge that led me back to God, and I can never repay you for that. You saved me. Thank you!

No longer anonymous,

Crystal Eldridge, FORMER Planned Parenthood Manager in Winston-Salem

FIVE

"Overcome Evil with Good"

It is true that we are in a war, and it is true that the New Testament likens us to soldiers in a battle (see 2 Timothy 2:3). But we fight differently than the world fights. As Paul told us, our weapons are supernatural, and our methods are from above, not below:

> For though we live in the world, we do not wage war as the world does. The weapons we fight with are not the weapons of the world. On the contrary, they have divine power to demolish strongholds. We demolish arguments and every pretension that sets itself up against the knowledge of God, and we take captive every thought to make it obedient to Christ.
>
> 2 Corinthians 10:3–5

Yet it is precisely in this way that we win the war. It is in this way that our revolution succeeds. After all, this was the strategy that worked for Jesus and for Paul and the rest of the apostles. It will work for us too!

Paul urged the Roman believers, "Bless those who persecute you; bless and do not curse" (Romans 12:14). Then he went on to write,

> Do not repay anyone evil for evil. Be careful to do what is right in the eyes of everyone. If it is possible, as far as it depends on you, live at peace with everyone. Do not take revenge, my dear friends, but leave room for God's wrath, for it is written: "It is mine to avenge; I will repay," says the Lord. On the contrary:
>
> > "If your enemy is hungry, feed him; if he is thirsty, give him something to drink. In doing this, you will heap burning coals on his head."
>
> Do not be overcome by evil, but overcome evil with good.
>
> Romans 12:17–21

The world fights with anger, intimidation, force, and even violence. We fight back with much more powerful weapons, overcoming evil with good, hatred with love, darkness with light, lies with truth, and the power of the flesh with the power of the Spirit. We also have the weapon of prayer, where we solicit the help of Almighty God, and we have the preaching of the Gospel, which transforms people from the inside out. What worldly weapon can compare with these?

Behind the Scenes of the Culture Wars

How does this work out on the ground today, in the 2020s, here in divided America? Let me take you behind the scenes on the front lines of the culture wars. In the third week of August 2012, Scott Volk, at that time lead pastor of FIRE Church, my home congregation, received a call from the local police to inform him that there would be a gay protest outside our building on Sunday morning. The leader of the protest announced on Facebook,

> We will meet just before Service begins, and protest as they gather, we will have a silent protest as service is going and let them have it as they leave for the day. Remember we will be peaceful and respectful, something they don't understand. We are going to STAND TOGETHER AS A COMMUNITY to show that our love is stronger than their hate.[1]

In response, I wrote this on my blog:

> On behalf of FIRE Church, I want to extend to you the warmest welcome and let you know that we are thrilled that you are here with us on Sunday. We have been praying for you for a long time!
>
> As always, you will only meet with love, kindness, and respect from the FIRE leadership and congregants, and we proclaim to you once again the amazing grace of God. Jesus died to save us from our sins, heterosexual and homosexual alike, and only in Him can we find forgiveness, redemption, and transformation. Jesus alone is the Healer, Savior, Deliverer, and Transformer.[2]

On my radio show, I also encouraged these protestors to come in good numbers so we could greet them and bless them. Scott posted a note on a local gay website that had announced the protest, in which he said,

As the pastor of FIRE Church, I just want you to know that you'll be greeted with the same love and compassion as we always endeavor to show anyone—you are more-than-welcome! You make mention of the "hate" that we show. Yet, in all our years here we've only desired to reach out with love to everyone in the local community here whether they are labeled as gay or straight. Hopefully, you'll see that love demonstrated on Sunday as you protest.[3]

Given the hostility, suspicion, and misunderstanding that existed between our two communities, Scott's gracious invitation drew some hostile responses. After all, in the past, members of our congregation and ministry school had lovingly shared the Gospel with participants at the annual "Charlotte Pride" event, and I had helped organize some of the counter-events. One year, about 500 of us gathered adjacent to the LGBTQ+ Pride rally, worshiping the Lord, praying, and confessing our own sins, all while wearing red shirts that said, "God Has a Better Way." We then distributed about 2,500 bottles of water to those at the Pride event, asking them if they wanted prayer for anything. And we had trained everyone with us to be gracious and loving in their interaction, making sure that our presence was in no way intimidating. Still, we had a very negative reputation in eyes of the Pride participants, and I had already been singled out online and locally as a homophobe and a hater.

Not surprisingly, the comments Scott received on the gay website where he posted his invitation read like this:

David: "Love is the most disfigured mask that hate wears."

Sue: "If what you think is reaching out in love is perceived as hateful attack, perhaps you should reconsider
your actions."

David: "You can fool yourself, Mr. Volk. You can fool your
parishioners. But you can't fool God. He knows what's in
your heart, and it isn't love. It's hate."

Tom: "What these fire church people probably don't
understand is that spending an eternity ANYWHERE
with them is what I would consider a true HELL. They
should concern themselves with their own pathetic lives
and leave others alone to theirs . . ."[4]

Scott responded by inviting the commenters to his
home for dinner and to spend an evening with himself
and his family. He explained that, "to call someone hateful without ever meeting them, seeing them, or hearing
them speak, is an indication of a heart that needs love. I
make myself available."[5]

On Sunday morning, August 26, about ten protesters
showed up. (We were disappointed that there were so few.)
Some of our FIRE leaders met them outside, offered them
water and snacks, and shared God's love and truth with
them. Then these leaders invited the protesters to join us
in the service. After a few minutes, however, the protesters left, explaining that we were too nice and too loving
to deserve a protest!

Bear in mind that these protesters knew the stands
we had taken for biblical values. Some of them had also
listened to my radio broadcasts or read some of my

writings. So they recognized how strongly we differed with them on many key issues. Yet they also recognized our genuine love for them and saw that we were not full of hate.

The next day, the leader of the protesters called my radio show to apologize publicly for the protest, explaining that their "anger . . . was aimed [in] the wrong direction." And then he said this: "Once we got there Sunday morning we were greeted with absolutely perfect love. I mean, it was fantastic."[6] Praise God!

I told him that I didn't feel he needed to apologize, since he thought we were a certain kind of people, but of course I accepted his apology. Then I told him, "The bottom line is that we both live here in the same city, and neither of us are moving from our convictions. How can we live as neighbors?"[7]

That question resonated with him as well. So after the broadcast, we exchanged contact information. A few weeks later, Scott and I had dinner with this leader and his partner, all four of us sharing our hearts graciously and candidly. And although things ended there, a powerful statement had been made.[8] Love speaks loudly and clearly!

About twenty-five years earlier, I heard a remarkable testimony from a friend of ours, who at that time was in her mid-sixties. She was a bright-eyed, silver-haired woman who reminded me of Barbara Bush, the wife of George H. W. Bush. She had a Ph.D. in biology and was on the front lines of the pro-life movement, participating in Operation Rescue events in which she and scores (or hundreds) of others would sit peacefully in front of an abortion clinic, praying and worshiping, until police arrested them and carried them away.

On one occasion, our friend traveled from Maryland, where she lived, to Buffalo, New York, to participate in a major Operation Rescue event. As always, she soon found herself arrested and sitting on a police bus, along with the other Christian women. But the police also made a mistake and arrested a zealous female abortion supporter, confusing her with the Christian protesters. Can you imagine how that lone woman felt sitting on the same bus with these other women, women whom she believed to be hateful and potentially violent? Our friend told us that the woman sat there shaking in fear, wondering what was going to happen to her.

The Christian women then began to reach out to her, sharing their own hearts with her, telling their own stories, and giving her the Gospel. That very day, she received the Lord and was born again!

This is how we overcome, not by yelling and screaming and by intimidating those who have tried to intimidate us. (I'm talking here about how we fight the culture wars. I'm not talking about how we engage in military battle with an invading enemy.) Instead, to repeat Paul's words, we overcome evil with good.

"From Deconstruction to Reconstruction"

The last week of February 2023, my staff forwarded a remarkable email to me. It was from Sarahbeth Caplin, someone I had previously interacted with when she was a hostile, "progressive" Christian writing for an atheist

This is how we overcome,
not by yelling and screaming
and by intimidating
those who have tried
to intimidate us.
We overcome evil with good.

website. Why was she contacting me now? (I share all this with you here with her full permission and blessing.) Sarahbeth wrote in her email,

> Dear Michael, This article recently came up in a Google search when I was trying to find something else I wrote . . .

The article she then referred to was one I had written on May 23, 2019, titled "Misrepresent and Demonize: The Weapon of 'Progressive' Christians."[9] Sarahbeth continued,

> It's so funny to read this now, because I no longer recognize the person you're talking about. At the time, I was going through a period of deconstruction. All the downtime in 2020 forced me to reevaluate everything I believe and why, and I'm happy to say I've returned to biblical orthodoxy—including in matters of sexuality. I just thought you would be interested to know that.

What great news! You can be sure I was quite interested to receive this report, especially in light of the article that she linked, which I had begun with these words:

> Last week, I encouraged Christian parents in California who had children in public schools to defy the law and pull their kids from the state's extreme sex-ed curriculum. How did the Friendly Atheist's resident Episcopalian blogger respond?
>
> According to Sarahbeth Caplin, I want these parents to teach "their kids that transgender people don't exist." (Yes, she actually wrote this.)
>
> In sum [she added back in 2019], "This is just faith-based, hate-fueled fear-mongering. It's the only subject in which Michael Brown is an expert."

What a sad commentary on the nature of liberal il-logic. And what a misrepresentation of the facts.[10]

And I ended the article with this appeal, to which I received no response:

> If the state wants to force trash like this on their children, then the righteous, moral, and responsible thing to do is pull their kids out of those classes.
>
> The only thing hateful is the response of "progressives" like Caplin.
>
> That being said, Sarahbeth, if you read this, let's talk. Join me on the air one day, and we can discuss the differences plainly but without vitriol.
>
> I'm willing if you are.[11]

That was then, with the old Sarahbeth. What happened to change her views so dramatically? What led to such a wonderful transformation?

When I inquired as to what had happened in her life, she shared this with me in another email (which, again, I'm sharing with her full permission):

> I'm not sure how the transformation started exactly, except that at some point I started praying for God to reveal the truth to me—no matter how uncomfortable it made me. And then I started noticing some inconsistencies within the LGBT movement: like how you're apparently "born this way," but at the same time, sexuality is also fluid? And for a same-sex attracted person to reject a trans person for a date is apparently transphobic (because the "parts" don't match the gender identity), even though, according to a sex-positive philosophy,

no one is supposed to be shamed for what they are into? That means the logic of gender ideology is actually homophobic! And it sort of spiraled on from there.

Sarahbeth continued, explaining to me,

> I realized much of my objections to Christian theology in this area were reactionary rather than based on scripture, so I started studying "the clobber verses" again with a more open mind. And once I finally understood them, I couldn't go back. Progressive Christianity is entirely built on doubts and questions with little to no foundation of certainty and truth. It was a temporary dwelling place for me to figure some things out, but ultimately not a healthy place to stay. And many of the "friends" I made in that circle dropped me once I started to regain my spiritual footing. They liked me when I questioned things and my faith was struggling, but not when I found it again.
>
> At that time, I stopped writing for Patheos [and the Friendly Atheist website]. . . . I have since joined the Anglican church (affiliated with ACNA, not the Episcopal branch), and have built a healthy spiritual community there.

In our subsequent interaction, she also wrote this:

> I reached out to you specifically because I probably sparred with you more than most, and definitely went out of my way to misrepresent your views. I was wrong to do that. I apologize for the version of me you had to deal with!

How many of us have the maturity to realize that we are reacting rather than processing, responding emotionally rather than based on truth? And how many have the humility—and integrity—to change course so dramatically after we have become known for espousing a particular position or being a particular person? Sarahbeth has that kind of maturity and humility. She detailed her full story on her website, in an article she titled "From Deconstruction to Reconstruction: a story of doubt to faith."[12] God truly does give grace to the humble!

And what a great summary of "progressive Christianity." As she wrote, it "is entirely built on doubts and questions with little to no foundation of certainty and truth. It was a temporary dwelling place for me to figure some things out, but ultimately not a healthy place to stay." This is the exact opposite of the real Gospel faith, which is built on eternal foundations filled with certainty and truth, foundations that have stood the test of time.

Let Your Interactions Be Full of Grace

My interactions with Sarahbeth also remind us of the importance of being gracious to those we differ with, even if our differences are sharp and require strong and clear articulation. As Paul exhorted, "Let your conversation be always full of grace, seasoned with salt, so that you may know how to answer everyone" (Colossians 4:6). This is part of how we overcome evil—and misunderstandings and false assumptions—with good.

We can be unashamed of our faith without being nasty, mean-spirited, demeaning, insulting, or self-righteous. And while we may sound impressive in our online echo chambers with our so-called boldness (which is really our spiritual justification for acting like jerks), in the end, we will only discredit the Lord with our ungraciousness and drive away those for whom He died.

To be sure, we will still be hated for the Gospel and for righteousness, no matter how humble and gracious we are (see Matthew 5:10–12; 10:22–23; John 15:18–20; 2 Timothy 3:12, among other verses). But let it be that, if we suffer reproach or insult or worse, we are suffering for the Gospel and not for our foolishness or fleshliness. As Peter wrote,

> If you are insulted because of the name of Christ, you are blessed, for the Spirit of glory and of God rests on you. If you suffer, it should not be as a murderer or thief or any other kind of criminal, or even as a meddler. However, if you suffer as a Christian, do not be ashamed, but praise God that you bear that name.
>
> 1 Peter 4:14–16

May we be identified with Jesus, and may we represent Him rightly to this world. Is there anything more important than that?

On August 19, 2023, I posted this on Facebook in large letters against a bright red backdrop: "If we want God's heart, we must humanize our opponents, not demonize them."[13]

One of those who responded was Sarahbeth, writing, "It worked with me."

That says it all!

SIX

Enrolling in Shared Humanity 101

My wonderful Jewish mother died on November 18, 2016, at the age of ninety-four.[1] She had lived most of her life on Long Island, but in her last few years we brought her down to North Carolina, where Nancy and I could help take care of her in her old age. The burial plot my father had purchased for himself and for her—before he died suddenly and unexpectedly in 1977—was in a Jewish cemetery in New Jersey. And so it was that immediately after she passed away, the funeral parlor director in North Carolina made arrangements to have her coffin brought to New Jersey.

The director asked me if we would like a rabbi to preside at the burial ceremony, so I asked my one sibling, my sister Melissa, for her preference. She requested a Reform rabbi. (Reform Judaism is the largest branch of Judaism in America, and also the most liberal.) But the local funeral director told me that there could be a potential issue with the Jewish cemetery in New Jersey because I am a well-known Messianic Jewish leader. (Messianic Jews are Jews who follow Jesus as the Messiah and who continue to identify as Jews.) Would a rabbi therefore have a problem with doing a service for my mother, let alone with having me participate in the service?

Shortly after meeting with the funeral director in North Carolina, I got a call from a rabbi in New Jersey. He told me he had been contacted by the cemetery personnel, who had asked him, "Will you have a problem doing the ceremony, since it's for Dr. Michael Brown's mother?" He didn't understand why this was an issue at all, so they told him again, "This is Dr. Michael Brown's mother."

That's when he realized whom they were talking about—*that* Dr. Michael Brown—and he assured them that he would be happy to conduct the service, letting them know he had no problem with "interfaith" services. He also wanted me to know—to my absolute surprise—that he was a regular listener to my radio show. When he missed it live on the air, he would catch it as a podcast later. How extraordinary!

I, for my part, told him to focus on my sister and her son in terms of the ceremony, since he would be there primarily for them. I would be concentrating on giving the eulogy, and I assured him that he need not be concerned about offending me in any way.

When we finished our talk, I got online to see if I could find out more about him. Again, to my absolute surprise, I learned that he was an out and proud, pioneer gay rabbi who strongly advocated for LGBT-affirming synagogues. I immediately texted him to let him know that I had read about him online and that it appeared our lives intersected in yet another unexpected way, making me all the more eager to meet him.

You might say, "But that's outrageous! How could you let a gay rabbi officiate at something as sacred as your mother's funeral service?"

Actually, the rabbi was there at the request of my sister and her son, so in that respect, the ceremony was for them. But from my perspective, it was altogether fitting that, on the day of my mother's burial, I would be standing side by side with an openly gay rabbi and that we would be treating each other with kindness and respect.

You say, "But don't you believe what the Torah says about homosexual practice?"

Yes, I certainly do, without apology. This rabbi, Bill Kraus, was fully aware of my position. Yet he, for his part, was quite willing to perform the ceremony for my mother, even though some rabbis once branded me "Public Enemy Number One" because of my Jewish outreach work, while some gay activists branded me one of the nation's "most vicious homophobes."

Fellow Human Beings

The reality is that Rabbi Kraus and I are fellow human beings, so what brought us together on that day was our shared humanity, our shared (albeit very different) Jewish heritages, and our shared commitment to honor the memory of the dead—me as a grieving son, and he as a hospice and cemetery rabbi. I truly believe all of this was ordained by God rather than coincidental. From my perspective, it illustrated what I have said for years: My opposition to LGBTQ+ activism is biblical, not personal, and I truly do care about those whose agenda I resist and whose "marriages" I don't recognize.

That's why I often recount that my first organ teacher, when I was just seven years old, was an openly gay man named Russ. He would often come to our house with his partner, Ed, a hairdresser. When they came to our home together, sometimes after Russ finished teaching my sister and me, they would stay for dinner. Ed would do my sister's hair. These are distinct childhood memories, and this reflects the openness with which our parents raised us. My faith in Jesus and my belief in the authority of God's Word has only deepened my love for those who identify as LGBTQ+, and only God knows the holy tension I live with in following the mandate to "reach out and resist," as I explained in chapter 3.

As for Rabbi Kraus, my greatest desire is that he comes to recognize Jesus as our Messiah. I imagine that one of his greatest desires would be to change my views about same-sex relationships. Perhaps that's why, some months after the funeral, he sent me pictures of himself with his partner and some of their shared grandchildren.

In any event, my mother's funeral service was meaningful to both of us, in that it provided an unexpected opportunity in a most personal (and painful) setting to demonstrate that, while we can be deeply entrenched ideological opponents, we are even more deeply committed to treating each other with kindness and respect. We can major on that ethical imperative without denying our theological and sociological differences. Isn't this a fundamental part of living in this world? Isn't this loving our neighbor as ourselves on the most basic level? Isn't this Humanity 101, let alone Gospel 101? (It's time we enrolled in these basic courses!) Isn't this something we do as families when we have meals together over the holidays, despite some deep differences we might have?

That's why Rabbi Kraus and I continued to text each other after the funeral. That's why he was kind enough to check on my daughter Megan and me to be sure we arrived safely home (she had traveled with me to New Jersey for the funeral). That's also why he assured me that his comments to his friends and colleagues about me were as respectful as my comments about him. He had heard me speak about him on the radio after the funeral, and he also approved of me writing an article that described what had transpired. Once again, the theme of the article was simple: *Humanize, don't demonize, those with whom you differ.*

More in Common Than We Realize

One of my radio guests was David Kyle Foster, a well-known leader in the ex-gay movement. Before coming to Jesus and experiencing radical and lasting transformation in the Lord, Foster had been a self-confessed drug abuser and sex addict. In response to his story, a woman called the broadcast, explaining that she was a lesbian in a committed relationship with another woman. Together, they were raising their children, to whom they were deeply devoted. Neither of them, she emphasized, ever got drunk, used drugs, or engaged in promiscuous sexual behavior. The kids, she assured me, were well-adjusted, healthy kids. As a result of her call, which was to combat the caricatured view of all gays and lesbians as crazed sex fiends, she and I had some private dialogue. She even expressed openness to the possibility of meeting me and bringing her partner. Her partner, having been raised in a Christian home, was more reluctant, yet still potentially willing.

What was clear to me was that this couple was, in most respects, just like any other respectable married couple, other than being a same-sex couple. They were devoted to each other, devoted to their children, were not living a wild life, not partying, not carousing. What was also clear was that this woman did not consider me to be a homophobe. Instead, to my great pleasure, I would sometimes see her post comments in my defense on our ministry's Facebook page, especially responding to what seemed like hateful, anti-gay comments. She would post something like, "Dr. Brown won't be happy to see this!" Or, "I bet Dr. Brown will have something to say about this." How remarkable!

To my regret, I failed to follow up quickly about us meeting together, and when I finally did reach out again, the door was closed. She was just too upset with the stands I had taken on LGBTQ-related issues, regardless of how I had taken those stands, so the idea of meeting face-to-face no longer felt safe for her or her partner.

I fully understood where this woman was coming from, and I simply attempted to leave the door open in the future, should she have a change of heart. But again, I regretted failing to follow up earlier. Perhaps, if we had had the opportunity to sit face-to-face, a lasting bridge could have been built? Perhaps, in the end, they could even have heard and received the message of the Gospel? The implications of the Gospel might have brought short-term pain, but the lasting results, in this world and the world to come, would have been glorious.

For the moment, that's all a matter of speculation. What's clear is this: We often have more in common with our ideological opponents than we realize. We share the common lot of humanity, the ups and downs of life. We share common goals—most notably, to live productive, meaningful lives. We share common experiences, from births to deaths, from hirings to firings, from successes to failures. And very often, those of us who are passionate for a cause share a deep desire to bring about positive change, which is why we clash so deeply. Our passions and burdens are on a collision course, and our deepest similarities reflect our deepest differences.

You might say, "All of that is fine and good. But why would I want to understand what I have in common with those who want to undermine what is most important to me? The way I look at it, that would only dilute the intensity of my convictions, if not even make me sympathetic to their cause. I say it's best to keep my distance and underscore our differences."

On the one hand, I understand those concerns, and I recognize that sometimes our sense of friendship with "the other side" can cause us to pull our punches, so to speak. That, of course, is a danger that we should be recognize and avoid.

On the other hand, it's essential that we understand our areas of commonality, of shared humanity, of similar hopes and aspirations and dreams. That's because this is the real world and this is a truthful assessment. Our caricatured views of one another are inaccurate and unhelpful, only fueling deeper fires of suspicion and miscommunication. How is this helpful?

Really now, how do we feel when our opponents do this to us? How do we feel when they demonize us, misrepresent us, caricature us, and talk past us? Does that help advance the cause of truth? Does that help clarify issues for those watching on the sidelines?

More fundamentally, do we appreciate it? Why, then, would we do to others what we would not want done to us? As stated in Judaism (in an earlier, reverse form of the Golden Rule), "That which is hateful to you do not do to another." Plus, when we speak about our opponents in caricatured, inaccurate terms, they recognize this immediately, and it indicates that we really don't know them at all. Or worse still, that we are blinded by hate.

I know it can feel safe to live within our little echo chambers. I know it feels reinforcing to have our views championed and affirmed and celebrated, without ever being challenged. But, to repeat, that's not the real world, and many of our caricatures and stereotypes simply are not true.

Gaining God's Heart Helps Our Cause

One of the most insightful recent books you can read, a book that exposes much of today's most radical ideologies—in particular, the pro-gay, pro-trans, anti-white, anti-male ideologies—is Douglas Murray's *The Madness*

When we speak about
our opponents in caricatured,
inaccurate terms,
they recognize this immediately,
and it indicates that
we really don't know them at all.
Or worse still, that we are
blinded by hate.

of Crowds: Gender, Race and Identity. Yet Murray himself is gay, openly and without shame. Another recent book that powerfully exposes the radical trans agenda is *Female Erasure: What You Need to Know About Gender Politics' War on Women, the Female Sex and Human Rights.* Yet it is written by staunch feminists, some (or most?) of whom are lesbians. It isn't only Christian conservatives who are speaking up against today's cultural madness.

Conversely, many conservative Christians have massive blind spots when it comes to other issues of social importance. How many of us were on the wrong side of segregation? Or think back to the founding of the Southern Baptist Convention, the largest Protestant denomination in the United States. Were you aware that it broke away from the Northern Baptists over the issue of slavery? Were you aware that the four founders of the famed Southern Baptist Theological Seminary were themselves slave owners who justified their practice biblically?[2] Perhaps we should lose some of our strut and learn to walk with more of a limp?

The reality is that many Americans live in a world where same-sex relationships are in many ways no different than heterosexual relationships, and many of these Americans in same-sex relationships are decent people, not radical ideologues. They find it utterly mind-boggling that people like us still debate this issue, let alone that we reject the idea of same-sex "marriage" entirely, to the point of using scare quotes to make our point (as I have done a little of here!). Does it help if we simply demonize them and write them off as supporters of perversion, or as perverts themselves?

The Bible is crystal clear on the subject of homosexual practice: It is always wrong in God's sight. And yes, we should have a righteous indignation against drag queens reading to toddlers and preschool teachers teaching trans ideology to four-year-old kids. And yes, we should oppose with all our might the genital mutilation and chemical castration of minors in the name of gender transition. Absolutely, categorically, unequivocally, and without compromise or hesitation. Yes! From these convictions, we shall not be moved.

At the same time, we only hurt ourselves when we fail to see the humanity of those with whom we differ, when we tear down, rather than build, bridges of communication, and when we contribute to the polarization of our society rather than working to bring people to God and His truth. Let us, then, get His perspective, and let us gain His heart. It will do us good, and it will only help our cause. We might even see radical change come to our society as we follow the way of grace and truth.

This is also what it means to have hearts of compassion and backbones of steel. This is also what it means to reach out and resist. This is what it means to be followers of Jesus in the midst of a hurting, broken world.

When I texted Rabbi Kraus, more than seven years after my mom's funeral, asking him for permission to use our story in this chapter, I was delighted when he immediately texted me back, writing,

"Thank you, my friend! You have my unqualified permission to use my name and our experiences on air and in print. My respect for your integrity transcends our positions on culture. I'd look forward to coming down to Charlotte and conversing with you on your program. And of course I shall order your book tomorrow. Kind wishes to you and your family for peace and happiness in 2024. B'shalom, Bill."

SEVEN

Hijacked by Demonic Forces

What comes to mind when you think of Antifa and BLM (or Black Lives Matter)? Do you think of young people seething with anger and hatred? Does your mind go to scenes of anarchy and looting and arson? Do you see cities on fire and crowds rioting in the streets? Do you think of radical Marxist ideologies baptized in openly queer, pro-transgender rhetoric?

If so, you are absolutely correct. Both these movements were fueled by carnal anger and gave vent to fleshly intimidation. Both movements were grounded in Marxist thinking and strongly rejected biblical authority. And both left destruction in their wake.

But that's only one side of the story. There is another side of the story, a side that's all too easy to miss in light of the chaos created by Antifa and BLM. Yet it is a side that has much to commend it, a side that even shares some biblical ideals—and I mean this from the heart.

Very few groups are completely and entirely evil. Very few movements are built entirely on rebellion and sin. Very few people have absolutely no redeeming qualities.

Of course, we could point to a radical feminist group like W.I.T.C.H. (founded in 1968), which was an acronym for "Women's International Terrorist Conspiracy from Hell." That certainly sounds downright satanic and evil! And the group did, in fact, stand for overthrowing what they perceived to be the patriarchal dominance of society.[1] But there's no doubt that among the women in this group were those who had suffered through abusive relationships, or worse still, rape. Their cause was wrong, but their pain was real.

It's the same with the "Shout Your Abortion" movement, which in my view is one of the ugliest manifestations of an anti-life mentality. There's nothing good about shouting your abortion or celebrating it in any way, let alone making light of it, as some in the movement have done. But here, too, the anger is often a mask for the pain some of these women carry, while the call to "shout" sometimes represents an attempt to drown out the silent cries within. And how many of these women were left pregnant after a one-night stand or a short-term relationship, with the baby's father nowhere to be found? In their view, how dare some religious fundamentalists force them to have that child while the father runs off scot-free and without a care in the world? "You better believe we will shout our abortion! It's the best thing we ever did" are some of the sentiments these women express.[2]

Going back in time to the 1960s, many young Americans (me included) were looking for more than the American dream. They were asking deeper questions about the meaning of life. The rapid changes in culture, the challenges to the status quo of the day, the shocking assassinations, and the specter of the Vietnam War created a deep sense of uncertainty, also leading to a spiritual search asking, *Why are we here after all?* A deep void existed in our hearts, one that led many of us to a transformational encounter with the Lord during the Jesus Revolution (also known as the Jesus People Movement, which began in 1967, when hundreds of thousands of hippies, rebels, and radicals around the world came to faith in Jesus).

Unfortunately, it was not only the Lord who filled that void for most of us during that time. Satan and the world rushed in to fill it, especially with sex, drugs, rock 'n' roll, and Eastern religion. That was the path many of us took before some of us came to know the Lord, a path from which many never returned.

And what did most Christian leaders see during the turbulent sixties? What did most churches perceive? Did they recognize that we young people were on a search, a deep and profound search—even a spiritual search? Did they recognize that behind our rebellion and anger and carnality was a deep cry for reality?

For the most part, the answer was no. That's not what most churches and leaders saw. Most of them only recognized what was happening on the outside—the immorality, the drugs, the rebellion, the wild lifestyles, the crazy hairdos and outfits, the new religious beliefs. As a result, even during the days of the Jesus Revolution, most churches still didn't realize it was harvest time, because of which the potential of this great spiritual harvest was not fully realized.

Seeing from the Outside In

We cannot afford to make this same mistake today. Instead, we must be able to see behind what is happening on the outside—the anger, the violent acts, the anarchy, the destructive ideologies, the anti-Christian rhetoric—and instead get God's perspective on what is happening on the inside. Is all of it evil and wicked? Or is there some positive motivation or ideal that has been hijacked by demonic forces?

In our modern day, as a young generation deals with its own set of uncertainties and frustrations, longing to see justice and equality prevail, Satan and the world have rushed in to hijack these sentiments too, many of which are good and noble in themselves. Nowhere is this clearer than in the hijacking of empathy, which is defined as the ability to understand and share the feelings of another person. It is partly because of empathy that a disproportionate percent of Gen Z'ers identify as LGBTQ+, even though only a small percentage of them are actively, let alone exclusively, involved in same-sex relationships and activities.

As a result, this quality of empathy, which can be very positive in and of itself, has been co-opted in a destructive, negative way. To give just one example, out of a deep sense of empathy with a marginalized person, many teens will instinctively defend the choices of a trans-identified peer, not realizing that this peer is about to destroy his or her life via chemical castration and genital mutilation. Rather

We must be able
to see behind
what is happening
on the outside,
and instead get
God's perspective
on what is happening
on the inside.

than lovingly helping their friend not to mutilate and alter the healthy body God has given him or her, their empathy moves them to side with an act of self-destruction. Their empathy in the short term actually contributes to their friend's long-term pain.

It is the same with the pursuit of justice and equality, in the name of which a male who identifies as female can compete against real females, not to mention share a locker room with them. Yes, this uncomfortable, unequal, and potentially abusive situation is justified in the name of equality. In a recent court case where a weightlifting association was ordered to "cease and desist" from banning biological males from competing against biological females, the verdict was reached in the name of fairness. It was determined that the association must not discriminate against a man who believes he is a woman—a judgment that thereby fosters discrimination against all true women.[3] What a travesty.

Almost twenty years ago, in April 2005, Dr. Al Mohler noted that,

> When Christian Smith and his fellow researchers with the National Study of Youth and Religion at the University of North Carolina at Chapel Hill took a close look at the religious beliefs held by American teenagers, they found that the faith held and described by most adolescents came down to something the researchers identified as "Moralistic Therapeutic Deism." [Remember that these adolescents, today, are in their thirties and forties.]
>
> As described by Smith and his team, Moralistic Therapeutic Deism consists of beliefs like these: 1. "A god exists

who created and ordered the world and watches over human life on earth." 2. "God wants people to be good, nice, and fair to each other, as taught in the Bible and by most world religions." 3. "The central goal of life is to be happy and to feel good about ones self." 4. "God does not need to be particularly involved in one's life except when God is needed to resolve a problem." 5. "Good people go to heaven when they die."[4]

Note again principle 2: "God wants people to be good, nice, and fair to each other, as taught in the Bible and by most world religions." In practice, this means, "If your religious beliefs or biblical standards offend me or cause me any discomfort, then they (and you) must be wrong, since they (and you) are not nice, and being nice is the essence of the Gospel." Add empathy to the mix, and you end up with this: "You and your religious beliefs are obviously wrong, since they make my friend feel bad." Add the pursuit of equality to the mix, and you end up with this: "You and your religious beliefs are obviously wrong, since they are unfair to my friend." This, in short, is the hijacking of empathy and equality.

A remarkable example of this can be found in a podcast dialogue between the social media superstar (and part-time professional wrestler) Logan Paul and his good friend and co-host, who is a professing Christian. Paul justified the open hostility he was showing toward his friend because his friend was a Christian and Christians believe in "conversion therapy."[5] That was it. Presumably, this alleged Christian practice made Paul's gay friends feel bad, and therefore Christianity itself was bad. Case closed.[6]

A colleague pointed me to a 2022 blog by Perry Glanzer titled, "Is Empathy a Christian Virtue? Comparing Empathy to Christian Compassion." While recognizing the potential value of empathy, Glanzer noted that,

> Indeed, surveys reveal that having greater empathy may lead to less sympathy for enforcing certain unpopular moral or legal principles on college campuses, such as freedom of speech. Empathy, in this case, becomes a weapon welded by those concerned about the feelings of the majority who are disturbed by speech from the minority.
>
> In this respect, empathy by itself is like a tool. It can be used properly or improperly. Whether it becomes the Christian virtue of compassion depends upon whether it is directed to God-ordained ends and results in action.[7]

This brings to mind a quote by author and philosopher Ayn Rand: "Pity for the guilty is treason to the innocent."[8] How easy it is to turn something good on its head! Those who reach out to the younger generation (and others who share their values) should recognize how some good values—some very good values—have been hijacked. And rather than simply reacting to the wrong positions the hijackers espouse, we can point them in the direction of *Christian* compassion and *biblically based* justice. Then, working together, we can take back what has been stolen and steer that passion in a positive, life-changing direction. It's called being redemptive. That's a virtue that is almost impossible to hijack, pervert, or twist.[9]

Looking Beyond the Obvious

As I mentioned earlier in the book, when God first called me to "reach out and resist" in 2004–2005, I spent as much time as possible interacting with the gay community. (I understand that, in fact, there is no more a "gay community" than there is a "straight community," so I use the term here in an imprecise way.) Not only did I make appointments to meet with local gay leaders, but I also engaged extensively online in blogs and other forums. I even accepted radio interviews in hostile settings, once doing an interview for a show based in San Francisco on "Queer Channel Radio." You can imagine how that interview went!

I also appeared on The Tyra Banks Show back in 2009, where, for the first time on TV, children who identified as transgender, some as young as seven or eight, were paraded on stage. There, together with their parents, they could tell their stories—and all of this was in front of a live audience. By the time I appeared for the panel discussion (which was three against one, me being the one), I was obviously the bad guy in the eyes of the audience—the big, very bad guy. I was the enemy. How could I change their hearts?[10]

But it was online, where people were not dealing with me face-to-face and many could hide behind their anonymity, that things got quite heated. People were angry with me. Very angry. My very presence hurt them. My words triggered traumas from the past, in particular for those who were raised in church. I was not just their ideological or theological opponent; I was seemingly the one who personally hurt them. They did not try to hide their outright hatred for me and my values.

Yet, as God is my witness, I didn't have to use self-restraint to hold back my own anger. I didn't need great self-control to harness my own rage. That's because I wasn't angry in the least, nor did I take people's comments personally. (For more on this, see the next chapter, in which we look at how to deal with rejection for the Gospel's sake.) That's because I understood that behind their anger there was pain, often acute pain, and my presence stirred up that pain again. My words opened up old wounds. That's why many responded with such vitriol and hatred.

To be sure, some people are just hateful, hating other people and hating God. Their venomous words come from an evil heart. Others simply lack all restraint. They lash out with the first words that come into their minds and quickly join the feeding frenzy of nasty comments. Still others demonstrate that they are children of darkness by rejecting the light when it shines. By all means, they must shut out that light before it exposes their sin and their shame. But, to repeat, some people speak with anger because it masks their hurt, and we must look past that anger if we want to reach those people.

Why do I bring this up in the context of asking if there is anything good in movements like Antifa and BLM? Once again, it's because we must look beyond the outward and the obvious, beyond the violence, beyond the burning of buildings, beyond the ugly rhetoric, beyond the deep-seated hostility. Is there pain behind the anger? Is there a longing for righteousness behind the deeply misguided zeal? Is it possible we are looking at people who, by the transforming grace of God, could be radicals for Jesus one day?

Having this perspective helps us respond in a godly way rather than react in a fleshly way. We can then employ biblical strategies reminding us that "a gentle answer turns away wrath, but a harsh word stirs up anger," and "through patience a ruler can be persuaded, and a gentle tongue can break a bone" (Proverbs 15:1; 25:15). That's why, when I was on the Tyra Banks show, I constantly stressed the words *love* and *compassion*, speaking them from my heart. I knew that I was going against the emotions of the crowd and the whole "pro–trans children" feel of the show. Only by emphasizing love and compassion, coupled with raising reasonable arguments and questions, did I have a chance of winning people over to the right side.

May the Lord use you as well to bring grace and truth together, and may you see the lost through our Father's perspective. Many of those who oppose us the most strenuously today will become our closest friends and co-workers tomorrow.

EIGHT

How to Cope with Rejection for the Gospel

Nobody likes rejection. Nobody likes being excluded or put out. That's because God created us to be social people, with families and friends and co-workers and teammates. That's why it feels good to be appreciated, to be accepted, to be valued, to be honored, to be respected.

In sharp contrast, rejection stings—often very deeply. What happens, then, when our friends or family members or co-workers reject us because of our moral and spiritual convictions? How do we suffer rejection, yet remain emotionally and spiritually healthy?

Here are some simple principles that will help you not only to endure rejection, but also to thrive and grow in the midst of it:

- Realize that it's not about you.
- Remember that it's a sacred honor to suffer for Christ.

- Know that others are experiencing horrific persecution for their faith.
- Keep in mind that love is concerned for those who are lost, deceived, or misinformed.
- Be aware that you are called to be a bright light—sometimes even a lightning rod!

Let's look at each of these principles a little more closely.

It's Not About You

The first thing you need to remember is that this is not about you. This is about the stand you are taking—for your faith or for a righteous cause. Put another way, the rejection you're experiencing is nothing personal and should not be taken personally. It's not an attack *against you* as a human being. It's an attack against the Lord you love, or against a cause that is dear to your heart. That's the reason for the separation and alienation.

Let's say you develop a circle of friends at your new job, and you all get along really well. You have meals together, your co-workers enjoy your company, and you get compliments like, "You're a lot of fun to be around," or, "I really appreciate how you take a personal interest in my life," or, "You're a nice person. I wish more people were like you." Wonderful!

Then one day, your friends tell you over lunch that they are so excited about an upcoming Pride event, celebrating LGBTQ+ diversity. "Do you want to go together with us?" they ask.

You tell them politely, "As a Christian, that's not something I celebrate, so no, I won't be going."

Suddenly, everything changes. The conversation quickly stops, and the rest of your lunch is quite uncomfortable, to say the least. It's also the last lunch you're invited to with your friends—or I should say, your former friends.

The rejection certainly hurts. It can even feel as if you've been kicked in the stomach. It sucks the wind right out of you. But in reality, this wasn't about you. This was about your convictions, values, and beliefs. As a person, the others liked you. It was your biblically based point of view that they didn't like, and that's why you got excluded.

It would be one thing if people didn't like *you*—your personality or your looks or something else about you. It's another thing entirely when people reject you because of your beliefs or values. That's when you stand strong. That's when you say, "It's worth it."

Or would you rather abandon your convictions and beliefs in order to keep people happy with you? Very few of us could live with ourselves if we had such a wishy-washy, spineless attitude. And don't we all agree that some causes are worth standing for, regardless of the consequences? Isn't there a feeling of dignity and even self-respect when you stand for something good and get rejected for it?

What if this was about your family? Let's say that your father had taken strong stands against segregation in the 1960s, and as a result, many racists hated him. Now, you've become friends with the children of those racists, but none of you is aware of that connection. Then one day, your friends learn you are your father's daughter. Immediately, they want nothing to do with you. At that moment, this is not about you. This is about your family honor. This is about your dad. This is about the good man he was and about the bad ideologies he opposed. Suddenly, that rejection doesn't sting the same way. Your perspective has dramatically changed. You will gladly suffer rejection for your father. To sell him out for the sake of new friends is unthinkable. The same is true of suffering rejection for your heavenly Father and His honor.

It's a Sacred Honor to Suffer for Christ

But the fact that it's not about us is just a starting point. The second principle takes us a little deeper and gives us even more courage and conviction. In short, we should consider it an honor to be treated the way Jesus was treated. It is our great privilege to be maligned and slandered and misunderstood for His sake. It is our profound honor to suffer the same rejection that the prophets of old suffered. It is actually a cause for rejoicing!

In Acts 5, the apostles were flogged and ordered not to speak anymore in the name of Jesus. Yet verse 41 records, "The apostles left the Sanhedrin, rejoicing because they had been counted worthy of suffering disgrace for the Name." What an honor! What a privilege! Their attitude was, "We've been whipped and have suffered disgrace for the sake of His name. Praise God!"

As Paul wrote to the Philippian believers, "For you have been given the privilege for the Messiah's sake not only to believe in him but also to suffer for him" (Philippians 1:29, ISV). Yes, it has been granted to us as a sacred privilege to suffer for Jesus. Thank You, Lord, for this honor! As The Message version paraphrases the same verse, "There's far more to this life than trusting in Christ. There's also suffering for him. And the suffering is as much a gift as the trusting." Again, thank You, Lord, for this gift!

In the early days of the Internet, I discovered a Jewish chat group that was devoted to countering the "missionaries" (Christian missionaries at large, but in this case specifically Messianic Jews who specialize in doing outreach to our people). To my absolute delight, I discovered that I was their biggest single target, and in post after post they maligned me and spoke evil of me. As I read their words, I was filled with an incredible sense of privilege and joy, running out of my study to tell Nancy about it. I was bearing reproach for my Messiah. I was being slandered for Him and because of Him. On some tiny level, I was being treated the way He had been treated. Oh, what a sacred honor! To be viewed by the world and treated by the world just as He was! Oh, what a joy!

As Jesus said to His disciples,

> If the world hates you, keep in mind that it hated me first. If you belonged to the world, it would love you as its own. As it is, you do not belong to the world, but I have chosen you out of the world. That is why the world hates you. Remember what I told you: "A servant is not greater than his master." If they persecuted me, they will persecute you also. If they obeyed my teaching, they will obey yours also. They will treat you this way because of my name, for they do not know the one who sent me.
>
> John 15:18–21

Jesus also said this:

> Blessed are those who are persecuted because of righteousness, for theirs is the kingdom of heaven.
>
> Blessed are you when people insult you, persecute you and falsely say all kinds of evil against you because of me. Rejoice and be glad, because great is your reward in heaven, for in the same way they persecuted the prophets who were before you.
>
> Matthew 5:10–12

And He said this:

> The student is not above the teacher, nor a servant above his master. It is enough for students to be like their teachers, and servants like their masters. If the head of the house has been called Beelzebul, how much more the members of his household!
>
> Matthew 10:24–25

Sometimes, the Spirit of the Lord actually comes upon us when we are suffering rejection or persecution for His name. As Peter wrote,

> Dear friends, do not be surprised at the fiery ordeal that has come on you to test you, as though something strange were happening to you. But rejoice inasmuch as you participate in the sufferings of Christ, so that you may be overjoyed when his glory is revealed. If you are insulted because of the name of Christ, you are blessed, for the Spirit of glory and of God rests on you.
>
> 1 Peter 4:12–14

During one of my many trips to India, Christians in the neighboring state had been suffering terrible persecution. Many had been beaten or killed. Thousands had fled their homes, and as a result lost their homes, taking refuge in the jungle. Church buildings had been demolished. I was even told that the local radicals would douse the wife and children of a pastor with gasoline, threatening to set them on fire if he didn't deny Jesus. Who can imagine demonic pressure like this?

A number of these persecuted believers were able to make the journey to the small conference where I was speaking. Each day, I did my best to minister words of encouragement and courage and hope, knowing what lay ahead for them. Also at the conference were young men who were about to go into that dangerous region to plant churches, along with two widows and one daughter of pastors who had recently been martyred. You can imagine how intense and sobering our times together were.

One afternoon during the conference, an Indian friend, one of the ministry leaders there, said to me, "The brothers are greatly encouraged. There is great joy among them. Your messages have really helped."

I asked him, "Why is that?"

He replied, "Because they are being treated just like the prophets of old!"

Yes! When you realize that you are standing in that same line, the line of those persecuted for righteousness or hated for their faith in the one true God, the line of the prophets and the apostles and the suffering Church worldwide, the line headed up by Jesus Himself, suddenly your perspective changes—dramatically. That sting of rejection now becomes a badge of holy honor. Praise God!

That's why it is so important that we conduct ourselves in a Christlike way. As Peter also wrote, "If you suffer, it should not be as a murderer or thief or any other kind of criminal, or even as a meddler. However, if you suffer as a Christian, do not be ashamed, but praise God that you bear that name" (1 Peter 4:15–16).

Others Are Experiencing Persecution

The third principle that helps us not become weighed down and discouraged when facing rejection is to recall that around the world, our brothers and sisters are experiencing horrific persecution for their faith. Every day of the year, some believers are killed for their faith. Some are beaten. Some are arrested and jailed. Some are tortured. Some are rejected by their entire families. Some lose their jobs. And we are going to get upset because someone unfriended us on social media? We are going to complain because our co-workers don't invite us out for lunch. Really?

We have a close friend who served as a missionary to Nigeria for many years. She's now in her sixties, a single woman who poured herself out for the poorest of the poor and worked in dangerous areas without backing down. She stayed and served as long as she could, even when persecution arose, until she was forced to leave her mission field because of changes in the government's visa policy. On December 3, 2020, I received an urgent email from this friend: "A Christian worker, a friend of my host, has just

When you realize
that you are standing
in the same line, the line
of those persecuted
for righteousness or hated
for their faith
in the one true God,
that sting of rejection now
becomes a badge
of holy honor.

been attacked by Fulani herdsmen and has suffered grave injuries from a cutlass. He has lost a lot of blood. Please pray. Thank you."

The next day we received the good news: "Thank you for your prayers. His wife reports that our brother is alive and currently stable. He has deep gashes to his head and is missing fingers. May God steady his heart, protect his faith, and heal his body."

This was a reason for thanksgiving. He had been badly wounded but was stable. Thank God!

If that had happened to most of us, it would be our story for years to come as we traveled from church to church and did interview after interview recounting our horrific ordeal. "They wanted to kill me, but the Lord rescued me! But you can see they cut off some of my fingers. And you can see this big scar in my head." Yet in my friend's world, where tens of thousands of Nigerian Christians have been killed for their faith in recent years, this was a positive outcome. The man was still alive.

Perhaps we could toughen up a little? Perhaps we could stop focusing on *our* feelings? Perhaps we could live as soldiers (see Paul's words to Timothy in 2 Timothy 2:3), recognizing that we are in a real battle and a real war? Read the words Jesus spoke to His prospective disciples in Luke 9:57–62 and other relevant passages, and then look in the mirror and say this: *By Your grace, Lord, this is who I am. I'm Your disciple. I'm Your servant. I'm Your soldier. I've been bought with a price, and I'm not my own. I don't have pity parties. I will follow You through thick and thin, come what may. It's an honor!*

In the Lord, you are stronger than you know—but you need to look outside yourself. There, you will find His strength working through your weakness. As Paul exhorted,

> Finally, be strong in the Lord and in his mighty power. Put on the full armor of God, so that you can take your stand against the devil's schemes. For our struggle is not against flesh and blood, but against the rulers, against the authorities, against the powers of this dark world and against the spiritual forces of evil in the heavenly realms. Therefore put on the full armor of God, so that when the day of evil comes, you may be able to stand your ground, and after you have done everything, to stand.
>
> Ephesians 6:10–13

So make this resolution: *No feeling sorry for myself today!* Don't underestimate the power of God's grace living within you. You are an overcomer!

Love Is Concerned for Its Opponents

Earlier in this chapter, we laid out the first principle in handling rejection, namely, to remember that the rejection we experience is not about us. It's about our beliefs or standards or convictions. But it's also not about us in another sense: As followers of Jesus, our concern should be for those who reject the Gospel or who are on the wrong side of an important issue, rather than being focused on how the rejection makes us feel. After all, love cares about the other person. Love is concerned that its opponents are lost or deceived or misinformed. That's where our focus should be.

Let's say that you're a medical worker sent out to an infected area with the cure for a deadly disease. Your assignment is to go from house to house, looking for those who are afflicted. When you find them, you are to identify yourself and say you have the cure. What a sacred mission this is. You will literally save people's lives.

What happens when someone opens the door and you identify yourself and state your purpose, but the person doesn't believe you? "Yes," this person says, "three of my family members are dying. But you're no medical worker. It's obvious that this is some kind of scam. You just want our money. Good-bye!"

Would you say to yourself, "That person hurt my feelings"? Would you say, "I'm going home to lick my wounds. They were very mean!"?

No. You would say to yourself, "These poor people! I have the cure for their disease. They don't have to die! How can I find a way to convince them? I've got to try again. Or maybe I can find a neighbor who can convince them."

It's the same with us and our message and the stands we take. We are trying to help people, not benefit ourselves. We are trying to do the right thing and save people's lives. If they reject us, we pray for them, we weep for them, and we look for other ways to reach them. That's what love does.

You Are Called to Be a Bright Light

Finally, it's good to remember that sometimes, we are called to be bright lights—in fact, lightning rods. That not only means that we draw the attacks and criticisms and rejection—that is certainly a big part of my own calling. It also means that our words or actions bring things to the surface. Now we see what's really in people's hearts, and often it is quite ugly.

But the redemptive side is that light is exposing darkness. Sometimes the more things get exposed, the easier it is to contrast the ugliness and anger and lies and venom with God's truth and love.

That also means that, if we are conducting ourselves in a Christlike way, sometimes the uglier things get, the better we are doing our job—and many others are watching too. Keep your composure, walk in grace, and some people will come out of darkness into the light.

My journal entry from May 24, 2012: "I get the amazing news from K. that I'm on the Southern Poverty Law Center list of 30 new activist leaders of the radical right—and I am pumped. On with it! God is confirming His calling on my life to be a revolutionary leader for His purposes. Making it onto the SPLC list today brings joy to my soul. God is giving me a voice!"

NINE

"The Lord's Servant Must Not Be Quarrelsome"

How do we deal with argumentative people without becoming argumentative ourselves? How do we address contentious issues without becoming contentious? How do we avoid needless quarrels and controversies when dealing with some of the most emotionally charged, easily misunderstood, life-and-death issues of the day?

How do we handle that family discussion over Thanksgiving, when the subject of politics comes up and everyone has a strong opinion? And what if we ourselves have the tendency to be argumentative and contentious? (That's certainly something I've had to deal with over the years.)

Paul gave the following counsel to Timothy, but it can be applied to each of us individually. He wrote,

And the Lord's servant must not be quarrelsome but must be kind to everyone, able to teach, not resentful. Opponents must be gently instructed, in the hope that God will grant them repentance leading them to a knowledge of the truth, and that they will come to their senses and escape from the trap of the devil, who has taken them captive to do his will.

2 Timothy 2:24–26

The Complete Jewish Bible translates verse 24 this way: ". . . and a slave of the Lord shouldn't fight. On the contrary, he should be kind to everyone, a good teacher, and not resentful when mistreated." The Message paraphrases it this way: "God's servant must not be argumentative, but a gentle listener and a teacher who keeps cool, working firmly but patiently with those who refuse to obey."

This is certainly a challenging calling, given how heated the issues can become, given how passionate the viewpoints can be, and given how contrary some people can be—not to mention our own fleshly tendencies to get hotheaded or argumentative. Yet this is what we are called to emulate, first and foremost as leaders in the Body of Christ, but also as believers. As Peter wrote to all of us,

To this you were called, because Christ suffered for you, leaving you an example, that you should follow in his steps.

"He committed no sin, and no deceit was found in his mouth."

When they hurled their insults at him, he did not retaliate; when he suffered, he made no threats. Instead, he entrusted himself to him who judges justly.

1 Peter 2:21–23

People may insult us, but we don't insult them back. They may rip us to shreds with their words, but we don't try to slice them in return. They may be snarky. We'll be sincere. They may hit low. We'll play by the rules. Yet once again, this is easier said than done, especially for people like me (and maybe you too?).

It's all too easy to quarrel and fight and argue, to debate in a carnal, nonconstructive way, to get caught up in the flesh, especially when others are in the flesh. Speaking personally, I have to be very careful here since I'm a debater by nature, by upbringing, and by experience. It comes naturally to me to debate and argue—quite naturally. I find it easy to be contentious, to push back, to refute, to challenge. And while some people run *from* controversy, I run *to* it. Does this describe you as well? If so, then you know that with the rise of the Internet in recent decades, bringing with it unfiltered, instant communication, we have to be especially vigilant not to become quarrelsome and contentious.

Is It Time for Kindness or Confrontation?

If you're like me, your first impulse is to confront rather than to seek understanding. If your verbal opponent strikes a blow, you want to strike back. And rather than looking for middle ground, you force things to extremes.

"You're wrong," the other person says.

To which you reply, "No, *you're* wrong. Totally wrong— 100 percent completely wrong."

People like that—like me, by nature—will escalate rather than conciliate. For us, conciliation is compromise. We will never do that!

People may insult us,
but we don't insult them back.
They may rip us to shreds
with their words,
but we don't try
to slice them in return.
They may be snarky.
We'll be sincere.
They may hit low.
We'll play by the rules.

What, then, do we do with these words of Jesus? "Blessed are the peacemakers," He said, "for they will be called children of God" (Matthew 5:9). And what of Paul's exhortation to the Corinthians? He wrote,

> All this is from God, who reconciled us to himself through Christ and gave us the ministry of reconciliation: that God was reconciling the world to himself in Christ, not counting people's sins against them. And he has committed to us the message of reconciliation. We are therefore Christ's ambassadors, as though God were making his appeal through us. We implore you on Christ's behalf: Be reconciled to God. God made him who had no sin to be sin for us, so that in him we might become the righteousness of God.
>
> 2 Corinthians 5:18–21

There is a time and place for confrontation and rebuke. There is a time when we stand our ground without compromise, holding fast to our godly convictions. At such times, compromise *is* cowardice. But there are other times when kindness, rather than confrontation, is called for. Times when it is meekness we need, rather than machismo. This is especially true when people have been taken captive by the enemy, when their minds are blinded and their perceptions blurred. This is when we need divine patience and supernatural longsuffering.

This is when Paul's words to Timothy that I quoted at this chapter's start come into play. But before we return to his wise counsel to Timothy, let's consider some other important scriptural passages. We are called to bring forth "the fruit of the Spirit," as outlined in Galatians 5, in contrast with "the works of the flesh" (see verses 19–21). Paul wrote, "But the fruit of the Spirit is love, joy, peace, forbearance, kindness, goodness, faithfulness, gentleness and self-control. Against such things there is no law" (verses 22–23). This breathes the very essence and spirit of our Master. As we emulate Him, the lost are drawn in. This is what the Holy Spirit produces in our lives. How beautiful!

Look also at James 3:13–18, reading each word carefully, as if you were tasting and digesting the choicest of foods:

> Who is wise and understanding among you? Let them show it by their good life, by deeds done in the humility that comes from wisdom. But if you harbor bitter envy and selfish ambition in your hearts, do not boast about it or deny the truth. Such "wisdom" does not come down from heaven but is earthly, unspiritual, demonic. For where you have envy and selfish ambition, there you find disorder and every evil practice.
>
> But the wisdom that comes from heaven is first of all pure; then peace-loving, considerate, submissive, full of mercy and good fruit, impartial and sincere. Peacemakers who sow in peace reap a harvest of righteousness.

Imagine what would happen to us if we prayed over these passages every day, reading them out loud (or memorizing them) and saying, *Lord, help me live this out! Give me that humility that comes from wisdom, that wisdom that comes from heaven. May these qualities describe my life, Lord!*

We can do the same with Paul's classic description of love, praying for these qualities in our lives as well. What a beautiful picture!

> Love is patient, love is kind. It does not envy, it does not boast, it is not proud. It does not dishonor others, it is not self-seeking, it is not easily angered, it keeps no record of wrongs. Love does not delight in evil but rejoices with the truth. It always protects, always trusts, always hopes, always perseveres.
>
> Love never fails. . . .
>
> 1 Corinthians 13:4–8

When I came to faith in 1971 at the age of sixteen, I had an extremely volatile temper and a very sharp, nasty tongue. I could be terribly cruel with my words, especially when I snapped and went on a tirade. And this bad temper did not disappear when I got born again. I had to learn to master it and rule over it (see Proverbs 16:32).

And as I sought to grow in the Lord, developing my character by His Word and Spirit, I developed the habit of praying some of these verses over myself every single night: *Father, Your Word says that love is patient and kind. Help me to be patient and kind! And help me, Father, not to envy or boast or be proud.* This is what I would do every single night. And notice that love is not easily angered! So I prayed, *Father, help me not to be easily angered.*

I would pray other passages over myself as well, including this one:

> For this very reason, make every effort to add to your faith goodness; and to goodness, knowledge; and to knowledge,

self-control; and to self-control, perseverance; and to perseverance, godliness; and to godliness, mutual affection;
and to mutual affection, love.

2 Peter 1:5–7

All of these qualities culminate in love! (See also Colossians 3:12–14.)

To Grow, Be Sure to Get Low

I can tell you firsthand that, as you spend quality time
with the Lord and as you sincerely ask Him for help and
grace, He will change you, just as He changed me. He will
answer your prayers. (He's still changing me to this day. I
have quite a ways to go.)

As you learn to get low and humble yourself when you
blow it, asking for forgiveness, welcoming correction, and
growing from your mistakes, God will continue to give
you grace. Put another way, if you want to grow, be sure
to get low.

That's why I marvel when people tell me how patient or
compassionate I am. Seriously? Me? The debater? The guy
who loves to argue? The guy who relishes a good verbal
fight? The guy who can easily be contentious? If the Lord
can change and help me, He can change and help anyone.

A few years ago, while I was speaking at a church conference in Texas, the pastor told me that he sometimes
gets really angry with gay activists who verbally attack
him and his congregants with foul accusations and ugly
attitudes. He asked me, "Do you ever get angry and want
to lash out?"

With total candor, I told him, "No, I don't. The Lord really helped me in that area."

He turned to a colleague of mine who was in the room with us, an old friend who had known me for years, and asked him, "Was this the way Dr. Brown used to be when you worked together?"

Without hesitation my old friend replied quite forcefully, "No!"

To the contrary, back in the day, I was the spiritual hatchet man, the one tasked with driving out those in our congregation who didn't belong. I was the one without patience for those who seemed undecided or wavering. In my view, you were either in or you were out, and you needed to make up your mind *now*. Pastoral ministry was not in my blood.

To be sure, I'm still not a pastor, and deeply compassionate people put me to shame. I often feel so shallow and insensitive, so quick to forget someone else's pain. Nancy is in a different universe than I am in this regard. The depth of her empathy exposes the shallowness of mine. And yet still, the Lord has taught me to be patient and kind. When it comes to caring, I really do try.

Can you relate to this as well? God will help us if we humble ourselves before Him, acknowledging our need and asking for His grace. He will actually change our demeanor from nasty to nice, and from cutting to kind.

Practical Takeaways from Paul's Counsel

With this in mind, let's return to Paul's counsel to Timothy. This time, we'll start one verse earlier, where Paul exhorted,

"Don't have anything to do with foolish and stupid arguments, because you know they produce quarrels" (2 Timothy 2:23). After explaining the types of things that produce quarrels, "foolish and stupid arguments" (the very things we can so easily get dragged into, or even instigate), Paul then says (my paraphrase), "As for you, Timothy, as a model servant of the Lord, be sure that *you* are not quarrelsome."

This, too, is often much easier said than done. Commenting on these verses, Professor George Knight explained,

> Paul has said (v. 23) that foolish and ignorant arguments produce quarrels (μάχας). He now immediately joins (δέ) to that the forthright comment that "the Lord's servant" himself must not be quarrelsome (μάχεσθαι). Paul then moves by contrast (ἀλλά) to three things that the Lord's servant should be: "kind to all," "able to teach," and "patient when wronged." Paul reverts to a more general and indirect way of speaking, referring to the "Lord's servant," which would include Timothy and others, rather than referring directly to Timothy as he has done in the previous two verses. He does this so that this instruction will benefit not only Timothy but also others who serve in that capacity (cf. 2:2, 14).[1]

So, as practical takeaways as the Lord continues to work on our characters, we should follow these holy guidelines:

1. Avoid foolish arguments. Watch carefully for these, and don't get pulled into a trap.
2. Be kind to everyone, especially to the unkind. After all, as Jesus said, "If you love those who love you,

what reward will you get? Are not even the tax collectors doing that? And if you greet only your own people, what are you doing more than others? Do not even pagans do that?" (Matthew 5:46–47). We're nice to nice people? Big deal. Anyone can do that. We're called to be nice to the not nice.

3. Keep our composure and watch our attitudes, not being resentful, staying patient, and remembering how longsuffering the Lord was with us.

As Paul wrote to Titus,

Remind the people to be subject to rulers and authorities, to be obedient, to be ready to do whatever is good, to slander no one, to be peaceable and considerate, and always to be gentle toward everyone.

At one time we too were foolish, disobedient, deceived and enslaved by all kinds of passions and pleasures. We lived in malice and envy, being hated and hating one another. But when the kindness and love of God our Savior appeared, he saved us, not because of righteous things we had done, but because of his mercy. He saved us through the washing of rebirth and renewal by the Holy Spirit, whom he poured out on us generously through Jesus Christ our Savior, so that, having been justified by his grace, we might become heirs having the hope of eternal life.

Titus 3:1–7

We should not slander others, remembering the foolishness we walked in before we knew the Lord and the unmerited grace that He poured out on us, bringing us into His very own family. We should show that same grace to others.

The great Puritan commentator Matthew Henry also offers these words of wisdom, expanding on Paul's counsel to Timothy:

> He cautions him against contention, and, to prevent this (v. 23), cautions him against *foolish and unlearned questions*, that tend to no benefit, strifes of words. Those who advanced them, and doted upon them, thought themselves wise and learned; but Paul calls them foolish and unlearned. The mischief of these is that they *gender strifes*, that they breed debates and quarrels among Christians and ministers. It is very remarkable how often, and with what seriousness, the apostle cautions Timothy against disputes in religion, which surely was not without some such design as this, to show that religion consists more in believing and practising what God requires than in subtle disputes.
>
> *The servant of the Lord must not strive*, v. 24. Nothing worse becomes the servant of the Lord Jesus, who himself did not strive nor cry (Mt. 12:19), but was a pattern of meekness, and mildness, and gentleness to all, than strife and contention. The servant of the Lord must be *gentle to all men*, and thereby show that he is himself subject to the commanding power of that holy religion which he is employed in preaching and propagating. *Apt to teach*. Those are unapt to teach who are apt to strive, and are fierce and froward. Ministers must be patient, bearing with evil, and *in meekness instructing* (v. 25) not only those who subject themselves, but those who oppose themselves.[2]

Let us never forget that at one time, we, too, opposed ourselves, fulfilling the desires of the flesh and the mind (see Ephesians 2:1–3). And, just as many of us were reached by the patience of God that other believers demonstrated to us—they were His representatives to us, His designated ambassadors—it is now our privilege to demonstrate that divine patience to others. May the Lord continue to make us like His Son!

TEN

Let's Have a Difficult Conversation

Abortion

Throughout this book, we've been talking about how our attitudes, actions, and words must reflect both grace and truth. We've used phrases like "reach out and resist," which means reaching out to people with compassion even while we resist godless agendas. We've emphasized the need to have hearts of compassion and backbones of steel. We've emphasized that there are two sides to every story, and we've acknowledged that all of us have blind spots. Now we've come to the point of the book where we flesh out these principles and actually have those conversations together—those important, difficult, controversial, emotionally charged conversations.

We'll focus in these next three chapters on three issues that we cannot (and should not) avoid: Christians and abortion, Christians and LGBTQ+ people and related issues, and Christians and race relations. How do we navigate these dangerous waters without crashing on the rocks—very sharp, very large rocks—that line both sides of the river? How do we keep God's perspective without becoming insensitive to people? And how do we maintain sensitivity to people without losing sight of God's standards?

As we launch into having these discussions, we'll start with the subject of abortion, putting the principles we have learned along the way into practice. In fact, I'll make the case *for* abortion as we begin this pro-life discussion. My goal is not just to play the devil's advocate in order to sharpen our debating skills. It's to help us feel the full weight of the pro-abortion argument, using very difficult, hypothetical scenarios to drive the point home, just as those of us on the pro-life side use the weight of late-term abortions to drive our point home. Earlier in the book, I presented some hypothetical, difficult scenarios. Let's expand on some similar scenarios here, giving names to the people in my hypothetical stories.

Is Abortion the Compassionate Choice?

Consider the story of a twelve-year-old girl whom we'll call Angela. She was abducted and raped by a sexual predator who had just been released from jail. Who can imagine her trauma? Who can imagine how this horrific event will impact the rest of her life? And how will it affect her whole family? But this is only the beginning. To add shock to shock, Angela finds out she is pregnant even though she is not yet a teenager. How can this be? As for the sexual predator, he raped two more girls before he was caught and will spend the rest of his life in prison.

The only positive thing is that Angela can get an abortion and put an end to the nightmare, without any of her friends and schoolmates knowing what happened to her. At least the horror can be hidden. At least her shame won't be broadcast throughout her school and her neighborhood. At least she won't have to put her young body through the trauma of nine months of pregnancy. At least she won't have to worry about giving birth to a child whose father was a serial rapist and child abuser. Abortion obviously seems the compassionate choice.[1]

Some of us, however, would forbid Angela that choice, imposing our morality and our religious convictions on her. And of course, those on the other side would respond, How dare we! How dare we impose our values on her—especially those of us who are men and cannot even relate to what a pregnant woman goes through in general, let alone a woman impregnated by rape, let alone a girl impregnated by a sexual predator? Who do we think we are? We are welcome to our religious convictions and moral values, but we have no business imposing them on others. Talk about smug self-righteousness.

You might say, "But a case like Angela's is the rarest of rare, with abortions performed because of rape or incest making up 1 percent of all abortions. What about the other 99 percent?"

That's a fair question, and there are some pro-life advocates who will accept laws granting exceptions for rape, incest, and, of course, saving the life of the mother, if that's the only way they can get any kind of pro-life legislation passed. At least those laws would address 99 percent of all abortions. But that still doesn't answer the question about Angela's pregnancy.

Abortion to Avoid Disabilities?

If it is wrong to say that Angela cannot have an abortion, what about another case that isn't so extreme? Let's look at a woman we'll call Donna. She is happily married to her husband, whom we'll call Tom. They have three children, the youngest of whom is severely autistic, putting lots of stress on the marriage and on the other kids. But Donna and Tom are devoted parents, and he has taken on extra work in order to pay for supplemental care for their autistic child. As for having more kids, that's not an option. First, they're in their mid-forties, a time when pregnancies can have more complications and where there are more potential problems for the babies, such as Down syndrome. Second, they cannot possibly handle another child, given how stretched they already are emotionally, physically, and financially. Consequently, they're very careful, using protection whenever they're together.

That's why Donna was so shocked to learn that she was pregnant at the age of forty-six. How did it happen? This was *not* good news for Donna and Tom. To the contrary, it was downright traumatic. Still, because Donna and Tom come from conservative religious backgrounds, they will not rule out the idea of having a fourth child, despite the difficulties involved. Perhaps they could even give the child up for adoption?

But things quickly go from bad to worse. Donna and Tom learn that the baby has severe disabilities and will not live for more than a few months. Not only so, but Donna will be at risk of a miscarriage the entire pregnancy. And then the baby will require day-and-night medical care if he or she survives the pregnancy. Worst of all, the baby's life will be marked by extreme suffering and pain.

Why on earth would these parents bring such a child into this world, only to have him or her suffer and die in a matter of months, most likely never even leaving the hospital? Why not save the baby, along with Donna and Tom, from devastation upon devastation? Surely, here too, abortion seems the compassionate choice. And who gives anyone else the right to dictate what these parents do with their child—or what this mother does with her own body and her own life?

Before you respond to these questions and say, "Yes, but it's a child, not a choice," please step back for a moment and do your best to put yourself in the shoes of Angela, Donna, and Tom. Can you see why they would think that aborting their babies would be a good thing, even a moral and compassionate thing? Can you sense their outrage at the idea that someone else—someone whom they've never met, possibly someone whom they voted against during the elections, possibly someone whose religious beliefs they totally reject—can tell them what decision they must make? "*You* are telling *me* what I must do with the fetus in *my womb*? Seriously?"

This is where we want to start if we are to have a helpful and constructive conversation—from the place of empathy and understanding, from the place of being able to say,

"I can't imagine what you're going through and what you have already lived through, and I don't pretend to know." Of course, women who have lived through the trauma of rape, especially those who were impregnated through rape, or parents who have agonized over the decision of whether to abort a severely disabled child, can speak with much more empathy. They *do* understand the pain.

The vast majority of us cannot fully relate, however, especially those of us who are men. How then do we start this conversation? How do we respond to the challenge of, "How dare you tell me what I can or cannot do!"? Before I point to some Scriptures that would be relevant for those who value what the Bible has to say, let me tell you two stories. One is about a man who has lived a long, full, and very public life. The other is about a tiny, helpless child. The man is named James, and he is past eighty years old as I write. The child is named Jude, and he is just nine. Their lives could not be more different, yet their stories overlap in many significant ways.

When a Life Is Saved

James has been one of the most significant Christian leaders of the last fifty years, leading multiplied millions of people to Jesus, first through his powerful evangelistic campaigns and then through his worldwide TV broadcast. His ministry has also provided humanitarian help to many more millions around the globe, serving the poorest of the poor in the midst of their hardship and suffering. He has also been a spiritual advisor to presidents, kings, and rulers, as well as to some of the most powerful

If we are to have a helpful
and constructive conversation,
we must start from the place
of empathy and understanding,
from the place of being able to say,
"I can't imagine what you're
going through and what you
have already lived through,
and I don't pretend to know."

businesspeople, educators, and celebrities on the planet, pointing them to the boundless love of God.

I'm speaking of James Robison, who has become a dear friend in the last ten years, pouring his wisdom and passion into me as well. *Yet James was conceived in rape.* As related by Penny Young Nance, CEO and president of Concerned Women for America (CWA),

> Robison's mother [who was 40 when raped] placed an ad in a Houston newspaper asking that a Christian couple care for her baby boy. A pastor and his wife noticed the ad and adopted Robison, who later, alongside his wife Betty, started the international ministry Life Outreach International.[2]

Would it have been better for the world if James had been aborted? Or did his mother make the right decision to bring him into the world?

Nance also notes this:

> Ryan Bomberger, founder of the Radiance Campaign . . . is among the one percent [of children conceived by rape or incest]. Ryan shared his personal account in an honest op-ed for LifeSiteNews, titled, "I was Conceived in Rape. Did I Deserve to be Aborted?" In it, Ryan thanks his birth mother for her decision to offer him life, writing, "My birth mother's courage to endure nine months of a traumatic pregnancy has had reverberations she never could have known. Adopted into a loving multi-racial family of 15 and now an adoptive father myself, I cannot ever express my gratitude to a woman who helped to defy the myth of the 'unwanted.'"[3]

How many other names can be added to this list of babies conceived by rape and yet whose lives are making a real difference today? (I immediately think of Jeri Hill, wife of the late evangelist Steve Hill, who is continuing his ministry until this day. Together, they brought a message of hope and salvation to millions.) And how many rape victims who aborted their babies subsequently realized that the abortion did *not* heal their pain? Some of these women have called my radio show to tell me this very thing: *Aborting the baby only made their pain worse*. In fact, according to Nance,

> In 2010, the Elliot Institute surveyed 192 women who conceived during a rape or incest (164 women were raped and 28 were victims of incest). Of those victims, 69% carried the baby to term and either raised the child or made an adoption plan, 29% had an abortion, and 1.5% had a miscarriage. They found that nearly 80% of the women who aborted said that abortion was the wrong solution; 43% of these women said they felt pressure to abort from family members or health workers.[4]

It appears that abortion is *not* the best way to make all the pain go away. In the words of one victim of rape, a woman who freely acknowledges the challenges of raising a child who was conceived by rape,

> I didn't consider abortion. . . . personally it felt that the act of killing the baby was actually going to make it worse, and that I would find that harder to live with than the difficulties that would be caused by having another child. . . .
> . . . I wasn't thinking about it from a moralistic view of not killing a baby. I was thinking . . . I would find it

harder to get through life dealing with not only a rape but then a termination . . .[5]

The ultimate issue, though, is even more basic. Let's go back to Angela, raped and impregnated at age twelve. Let's say that she carried the baby to term and then gave birth to a healthy child, but every time she and her family saw the child, they were traumatized. Would it be right to throw the baby away? Would it be right to kill the little child? Every person I know would say, "Absolutely not! That would be murder."

So, the real question is this: When does the "fetus" become a child? If you say the moment it is born, then you're saying that a totally viable baby, fully developed and ready to live and thrive outside the womb, is actually not a child, thereby justifying the most barbaric forms of late-term abortion. But once you realize that at the moment of conception the baby received its full, incredibly complex, intricately detailed DNA coding, you realize that you're dealing with human life from the start.

And think of how a woman feels when she finds out that, after years of trying to have a baby, she is finally pregnant. "We're having a baby!" she exclaims. And when the baby kicks for the first time, she says to her husband, "Honey, put your hand on my stomach and feel the baby kick!" (Notice she doesn't say, "Honey, come feel the fetus kick!") She might even start talking to her baby—before she even has a baby bump (not a fetus bump!). As soon as she finds out whether it's a boy or girl, she and the father start talking about what to name their child. And you can be assured that they do *not* say, "What should we name the fetus?" Instead, it's, "What should we name our baby?" (That's why the mother will also have a baby shower, not a fetus shower.) Yet all this time, technically speaking and using precise medical terminology, the baby is called a fetus. Yes, the fetus is an unborn child, not a mass of cells or a clump of carbon. That really is a child in there, and no one has the right to deprive that child of the opportunity to live.

The questions, then, are these when it comes to Angela's situation: Is it right to punish the child for the terrible sins of the father? Could it be that giving birth to the baby, even for the purposes of adoption, will bring more healing to the mother—the victim of rape—than aborting the child? And is it possible that God could bring good out of evil? That out of the horrible crime of rape, a human being could be born who could enrich the lives of many others? Could it be that snuffing out the child before he or she has a chance to live is actually snuffing out the only real way to bring something positive out of this tragedy?

Everyone Has Something to Offer

This time I'll tell you the story of Jude, which we can relate back to the agonizing choice that Donna and Tom need to make. Jude is now nine years old, and his parents faced a similar choice. He has not spoken a single word in his life. He weighs just 22 pounds and is only 24 inches long, wearing clothes for babies ages 12 to 18 months. He has been hospitalized too many times to count and has been given over to die since he was in the womb. In fact, it was during the baby shower, while he was in his mother Hannah's womb, that she began to bleed profusely and had to be rushed to the hospital. She almost lost him then, and it was touch and go throughout her entire pregnancy, meaning that she had to change her lifestyle and drastically restrict her activities if the baby was to survive.

It was only then, during the pregnancy, that Hannah and her husband, Sully, learned that they both carried a rare genetic marker. Because of this marker, as a couple there was always a chance that they could have a child with severe abnormalities—in this case, a child with an extremely rare condition known as Rhizomelic chondrodysplasia punctata (RCDP), a childhood disease with no known treatment. They were told it was highly unlikely that the baby would survive the pregnancy, and if he lived, his life would be very short and very traumatic. Even so, if he managed to live for several months or even a year, he would be utterly helpless and virtually noncommunicative. Surely, abortion was the merciful path to take.

But Jude's mom and dad were committed Christians, firmly believing that God was the author of life and that He had breathed life into the child in her womb. Abortion was not an option. So Hannah survived a very difficult pregnancy, almost losing Jude several times along the way, and confined to bed for much of the pregnancy. And to this moment, Jude requires constant medical care, either from his mother or grandmother or a nurse—and I mean every single day of his life.

When I asked Hannah if Jude was able to use his limbs at all or communicate, she replied, "Jude is nonverbal but loves to laugh and communicates with us in his own special ways. He has very little movement in his arms and legs and is therefore wheelchair dependent. However, he shakes his head back and forth when he is laughing and happy. And he loves to hold balloons in his hands, which encourages him to move his arms in therapy and playtime."

Jude has endured endless seizures, endless hospitalizations, endless doctor's visits, and endless treatments. Yet he lives on, a rare long-term survivor with his condition. *And Hannah and Sully say that Jude is the greatest blessing God has given to them.* His grandparents say the same thing. Jude has literally brought hope and encouragement and faith to countless people around the world, with more than 100,000 Facebook followers.[6] His grandparents on his mother's side are close friends of mine, and they have shared amazing stories with me about the effect of Jude's life, including letters they have received from women who were about to abort their own babies before hearing his story. They even heard from a pastor who had fallen away from the Lord and lost his faith, but came back to the Lord because of Jude. How incredible.

I was talking with his grandparents after one of those times when Jude had just endured another difficult hospitalization and almost died. I asked them, "Do you ever pray that the Lord would end his suffering and take him home?" They lovingly rebuked me for my question. That was their precious grandchild. That was their children's baby. That was a precious human life, someone who brought hope and life to many others. Of course they didn't feel that way. Instead, they continued to thank God for Jude and to pray that God would heal him. They recognize that every year of his survival marks another miracle.

The point of all this is to say that the most fragile, most severely disabled human being is of infinite value in God's sight and has something to offer this world. That's why we don't throw disabled or deformed babies into the trash. God forbid! To the contrary, if we have any decency inside us, every fiber of our being shouts out, *Take special care of those little babies and children. Take care of those severely disabled adults. Take care of those suffering elderly people who cannot take care of themselves. Take up their cause!*

That's why all of us, whether we are pro-life or pro-choice, recoil at the actions of the Nazis, who first discarded the elderly and the weak, euthanizing the mentally and physically impaired, eliminating those who did not live up to their standards and ideals. After all, the Nazis thought, of what use to society are they?

One of the most sacred events I ever participated in took place years ago in India, where I was presiding at the graduation ceremony of a close friend's ministry school. Soon, the graduates would be sent out to tribal regions to plant new churches, and I had the joy this day of speaking at their graduation and handling out their diplomas. This was our custom every year. But this time, I also had the privilege of handing out diplomas for another school my Indian friend had started. This program was for severely disabled people, men and women who couldn't use their legs or their hands or were blind. Yet each of them received special training, learning a skill by which they could earn a living, despite their physical challenges. I'll never forget their beaming smiles as they made their way onto the platform to receive their diplomas, some of them barely able to walk, reaching out a twisted hand to shake mine, or needing to be helped by others because of their disabilities. I truly felt it was one of the greatest honors of my life, especially knowing that, without my friend's help, these precious people might have been consigned to a life of terrible suffering, sleeping on the streets and begging for food just to survive another day. Should we just discard them?

A pro-choice advocate might reply, "But isn't it much better to stop the suffering before it happens, to save the child from a miserable life?"

In response, I would reply that first, you're saying it would have been better to terminate someone like Jude in the womb. His mom and dad, his extended family, and tens of thousands around the world would shout back, "*Never!*" Second, at what point do we draw the line? What if the baby would be born blind, but otherwise healthy? Or be born lame, but otherwise healthy? Or be born with some other life-hindering, but not life-ending condition? Do you see where this kind of thinking can lead? And do you see how, in incremental ways, it feeds into the destructive mentality that only the healthiest and fittest have a role to play in society?

Sadly, today in the country of Iceland, there are almost no children with Down syndrome—but not because of an incredible medical breakthrough that has eradicated the condition. Instead, it is because of abortion.[7] These weaker ones have been weeded out. The thought there is that it's best not to bring them into the world at all!

In stark contrast with this attitude, one article on a study of families that include a Down syndrome child reported,

> Families of children with Down syndrome face challenges, but by and large their experiences are positive ones, a new study suggests.
>
> Researchers found that in 87 percent of families they surveyed, everyone—parents and siblings—said they loved their family member who had Down syndrome, and almost as many families said they felt pride for the child.
>
> Few families expressed any regret about having a child with Down syndrome, the researchers reported in the April issue of the *American Journal of Medical Genetics Part A*.[8]

Not only so, but reports indicate that children (and adults) with Down Syndrome self-report as happy. This caused pro-life leader Jeanne Mancini to ask in a perspective she shared in the *Washington Post*, "People with Down syndrome are happy. Why are we trying to eliminate them?"[9]

Adding in the Scriptures

I share all of this to say that the baby conceived in rape and the severely disabled baby are babies still, and just as we would not discard them after birth, we should not discard them before birth. And people like James Robison, and like little Jude, remind us that God is a redeemer, bringing good out of evil and healing out of pain. Deciding to have that child rather than terminate it could be the most life-giving, life-affirming, life-restoring thing that Angela or Donna could do.

When we add in the scriptural testimony that indicates that the baby in the womb has life and destiny and purpose—yes, even while still in the womb—and has been carefully made by our Creator, we realize that abortion, however compelling the argument might seem, is not the best or most compassionate option. Here are two such Scriptures to consider:

> The word of the LORD came to me, saying,
> "Before I formed you in the womb I knew you, before you were born I set you apart; I appointed you as a prophet to the nations."
>
> Jeremiah 1:4–5

> For you created my inmost being; you knit me together in my mother's womb. I praise you because I am fearfully and wonderfully made; your works are wonderful, I know that full well. My frame was not hidden from you when I was made in the secret place, when I was woven together in the depths of the earth. Your eyes saw my unformed body; all the days ordained for me were written in your book before one of them came to be.
>
> Psalm 139:13–16

See also passages like Genesis 25:19–23, Luke 1:39–45, and Galatians 1:15. These Scriptures show us that there is a better way. Life is the better way since God has given every child, even while in the womb, a destiny.

Mapping Out Your Conversation

Now let's look at a summary of the issues surrounding abortion. On the left in the table that follows, you'll find the pro-choice perspective, which we need to understand if we're to reach out to the people who hold such a perspective, while resisting their agenda. On the right you'll find the pro-life perspective, which will help you respond to the issues with a compassionate, yet godly and informative, reply. Beyond that, to finish our discussion on this issue, you'll find thought-provoking "Questions to Ask" that you can introduce into the discussion when you are having this difficult, but vitally important, conversation with others.

Summary of Issues

Pro-Choice Issue	Response
Abortion is the compassionate choice. It ends the nightmare and saves the woman and her family from the shame, and her body won't have to be put through the trauma of nine months of pregnancy. At least she won't have to worry about giving birth to a child whose father was a rapist or a child abuser.	Abortion does not take the pain away. Most victims who abort their babies subsequently realize that abortion does *not* heal their pain. A study found that nearly 80 percent of the women who aborted said afterward that it was the wrong solution.

Pro-Choice Issue	Response
It's only a fetus, not a baby.	When a woman is pregnant, she does not say to her husband, "Wow, I just felt the fetus kick." They call it a baby because they know that's what it is. Science shows that three weeks after conception, the baby's heart begins to beat with his or her own blood. Five weeks later every organ is present, and the fetus clearly looks like a small-scale baby.
It is terribly cruel to force a victim of rape to carry to full term, then give birth to a baby conceived in an act of violence by a hostile stranger. Who gave anyone the right to impose their morality on a victim of rape? Every moment of her pregnancy is another reminder of her suffering and pain, while terminating the pregnancy is a way to end the pain. And for the mother to look into the eyes of a child conceived in rape is to see a reflection of the rapist. How can this be fair?	The child should not be punished for the father's sins. Giving birth to the baby, even for the purpose of adoption, can bring more healing to the mother—the victim of rape—than aborting the child. God can bring good out of evil and a human being can be born who can enrich the lives of many others. Snuffing out the child before he or she has a chance to live is actually snuffing out the only real way to bring something positive out of this tragedy.
It is much better to stop the suffering before it happens and to save the child from a miserable life.	The most fragile, most severely disabled human being is of infinite value in God's sight and has something to offer this world.

———— Questions to Ask ————

- Why do you feel so strongly about abortion?
- Have you, or has someone close to you, struggled with the issue of abortion?
- How does abortion take the pain of a traumatic or difficult scenario away? How does abortion create a new set of problems?
- Do you know when a baby in the womb has a heartbeat?
- If abortion was allowed for rape and incest, would you make other abortions illegal?
- Should a child be punished for the parents' mistakes?

ELEVEN

Let's Have a Difficult Conversation

LGBTQ+

Let's shift in this chapter to one of the most contentious and difficult moral and spiritual questions of the day, the question of LGBTQ+. Once again, I want to present some pro-LGBTQ+ perspectives before sharing my response. This way, I'm doing my best to help Christian conservatives see the world through the eyes of those who identify as gay or bi or trans (or other).

As I did in the previous chapter, I'll again use a hypothetical, yet very realistic example here as we begin this challenging discussion. Except this time, the issues involve LGBTQ+ individuals and their activities and concerns. And this time, I'm going to involve you in the story.

Great Guys with Homosexual Attraction

Imagine that your cousin, whom we'll call Alan, is one of the nicest people you know. He is a few years older than you, but as long as you can remember, he has always paid attention to you at family gatherings, and he treats you like a peer. After his mom and dad divorced (his dad is your mom's brother), the family gatherings became a little more complicated. But Alan stayed in touch with you, and once you were in college, you and Alan had some very candid discussions.

Alan respects your faith, even though he himself is not much of a believer in God, and he knows you hold to conservative morality when it comes to sex and marriage. But as far back as he can remember, he was never attracted to the opposite sex, always feeling a little different than his friends. Homosexual attraction for him seemed as natural as heterosexual attraction does for you. Yet like you, he didn't sleep around, he didn't like some of the lewd displays at gay pride events, and for quite a few years, he has been in a solid, committed relationship. In fact, his partner, whom we'll call Tim, is a really nice guy too.

Alan and Tim don't drink or use drugs. They are hardworking, decent human beings. Yet until 2015, no matter how many years they spent together, the government would not recognize their relationship because they could not marry.

You say, "But that's the whole problem. Marriage, by its very definition, is the union of one man and one woman. Plus, God didn't design men to be with men and women to be with women."

Alan would say in reply, "Says who? I'm not even sure God exists, let alone cares about the details of my love life. I would imagine that if this God really does exist, a God who created the entire universe, He'd have a lot bigger fish to fry than what my partner and I do in private. And I can tell you that for Tim and me, this *is* how we were designed—to love each other, to support each other, to care for each other, and to make the world a better place together. What's so bad about that?"

Alan continues: "After all, we live in a free country where we can choose our paths in life, regardless of our race or religion, and where you can have your beliefs and values and I can have mine. As long as we don't break the law, we are free to decide whether or not we marry and whom we choose to marry. So are you really going to tell me that because of some teachings in the Bible—an ancient book with lots of odd stories and embarrassing passages—that Tim and I can't marry? Is that really your place?"

But Alan isn't finished. "The fact is," he says, "Tim and I recently adopted a troubled child, an orphan whom no one else would take in. She had bounced around the foster care system, getting more troubled each year, then finally wound up back in the orphanage until Tim and I gave her a home—a stable, loving home, for the first time in her life. Are you going to tell me that God disapproves of this just because our sexual expressions in private might be different than yours? Is that really what you believe?"

It would be one thing if Alan were a militant gay activist working hard to marginalize Christians like you and even put you in the closet. Or if he were one of those super-promiscuous gay men who have dozens of anony-mous sexual encounters. Or if he were a woman, in this case a lesbian, riding her motorcycle topless at the local gay pride event while celebrating "nipple freedom," boast-ing about how she's on the lookout for "dykes on trikes." It's easy for us to raise moral and religious objections to examples like this. But how do we respond to the case of Alan and Tim? Simply stating "my Bible says that homo-sexuality is an abomination" isn't going to do the trick.

I should also point out that if you're a Gen Z reader, you probably feel that empathy is a very important qual-ity, and you recognize how important it is to side with the outcast, with the underdog, with the marginalized. That's why you probably grew up defending the trans kid in your class who got bullied, or the gay kid whom the other boys called a sissy. You felt it was right to stand up for them, and now that they're adults, you feel it's important that they can be who they want to be and live how they want to live. That, for you and your peers, is the proper moral position. I ask again, how then do we respond?

Let's also remember that in the case of Alan and Tim, their lives are quite similar to the lives of many hetero-sexual couples. They go to work. They go to the gym (although not as often as they would like). They enjoy watching a movie together or playing board games. They have a circle of friends with whom they have meals or do fun activities. And they have their good days and their bad days, along with some ups and downs in their relationship. The only thing that really distinguishes them from others is how they have sex in private—which is no one else's business. So I ask again, how do we respond?

Unpacking the Issue of Trajectory

What we really need to do is demonstrate that God prohibited homosexual practice because He is good, not bad, because He knows what is best for human flourishing, and because He sees where our decisions and choices ultimately lead. He sees the trajectory in advance. In other words, there really is such a thing as a slippery slope, and once we start sliding, it's very hard to stop. We also need to emphasize that once the law rules on a matter (in this case, on the redefining of marriage), then it *does* impact everyone else, like it or not.

Let me unpack these points one at a time, starting with the issue of trajectory. In May 2023, the articulate gay journalist Andrew Sullivan penned a major essay titled, "The Queers Versus the Homosexuals." Looking back at the last forty years, Sullivan noted that the survivors of the AIDS epidemic "built a movement that won every gay and lesbian the right to be free from discrimination and to marry and serve openly—and proudly—in the military."[1] He continued,

> It was the most speedily successful civil rights story in memory. Its case for equality was simple and clear: including us in existing institutions needn't change anything in heterosexual life. 'Live and let live' in equality and dignity was the idea. And the most powerful force behind this success was the emergence of so many ordinary gays and lesbians—of all races, religions, backgrounds, classes, and politics—who told their own story. America discovered what I had discovered the first time I went into a gay bar: these people were not the stereotypes I was told about.

They were not some strange, alien tribe. They were just like every other human, part of our families and communities; and we cared about each other.[2]

Unfortunately, Sullivan explained, the movement had veered from its original purposes, now including the T and the Q along with the LGB. He makes the point,

> But when you examine the other issues at stake—public schools teaching the concepts of queer and gender theory to kindergartners on up, sex changes for children before puberty, the housing of biological males with women in prisons and rape shelters, and biological males competing with women in sports—you realize we are far beyond what the gay rights movement once stood for. It's these initiatives from the far left that are new; and the backlash is quite obviously a reaction to the capture of the gay rights movement by queer social justice activists.[3]

Worst of all, these queers, says Sullivan, are now targeting children, "something," he writes, "we gays never did."[4] Sullivan, in turn, would be joined by groups like Gays Against Groomers as they raise their voices in protest against things like Drag Queen Story Hour, where drag queens read stories to toddlers and little children, with the enthusiastic approval of the American Library Association.[5]

Unfortunately, with all respect to Sullivan and groups like Gays Against Groomers, you cannot separate the LGB from the T and Q. First, gay activists have most assuredly targeted children for decades, particularly in children's education, as I documented at length already in 2011 in my book *A Queer Thing Happened to America*. They may not have targeted children's bodies the way trans activists have, but they have surely targeted their hearts and minds.[6] Their intentions may have seemed praiseworthy from their perspective, as they sought to protect LGBTQ+ identified kids from discrimination or mistreatment, and as they attempted to help these kids accept their identities at younger ages. But the results have been disastrous, resulting in massive confusion in the youngest generation.[7]

Second, the progression from LGB to T and Q is inevitable, a natural part of the deviation from the God-established, biologically essential, heterosexual norm. The long-predicted slippery slope was not a figment of the imagination of the radical, fundamentalist, fear-mongering, bigoted, Christian right. It was a logical, biblically based deduction. That's why the last chapter of *A Queer Thing Happened to America* was titled, "GLBT and Beyond: Reflections on Our Current Trajectory." And that's why the chapter opened with quotes like these: "In recent years gender identity has galvanized the queer community perhaps more than any other issue. The questions go beyond the nature of male or female to a yet-to-be transverse region that lies somewhere between and beyond biologically determined gender."[8] And this: "We are transgendered men (female-to-male, or FTM). My boyfriend is the mother of my child."[9] And I wrote this, warning about what was coming:

> There are massive and costly consequences to this deviation from the basic, male-female ordering of human life and society, and so, before we proceed any further—and

with due respect to the many legitimate questions that must be addressed, including how to help . . . troubled [and suicidal] gay and lesbian teens . . . we should first look ahead and see where we're headed. In fact, the future is already here: Welcome to a queer new world![10]

I also noted that,

Already in 2001, Richard John Neuhaus could write: "'The Transgender Revolution' is the latest political cause being promoted by those of heightened consciousness. Columnist John Leo notes that San Francisco now pays for city employees who want sex-change operations, and a number of television shows are in the works portraying the joys of transgendered liberation. The *Los Angeles Times* had a sympathetic story on a husband and wife who are both having the operation. They will stay married, but the husband will become the wife and vice versa.[11]

That's why I warned, "Yes, from 'transgendered liberation' to husband and wife swapping in the same marriage (!), we have entered some unchartered territory. We had better think twice before we proceed."[12]

In short, there *is* an inevitable trajectory of deviating from biological and societal norms, and this has nothing to do with bigotry or hate. It is as simple as saying, "If you eat junk food on a daily basis, your health will eventually be impaired," or, "The children of alcoholics have a much higher likelihood of becoming alcoholics than the children of non-alcoholics."

When it comes to biological design, it's hard to argue with the fact that men were made for women and women for men, and I say that to you whether you believe in evolution, divine creation, or a combination of both. Only males and females can reproduce. Only biological men have sperm, and only biological women have eggs. Only a biological woman can conceive and nurse a baby. Even in sexual functioning, our bodies are designed to work properly with heterosexual acts more than with homosexual acts. Again, this is biology, not bigotry.

When it comes to parenting, moms and dads are different and unique in ways that are far beyond the uniqueness of two different men or two different women. That's why the world's best dad is not a mom and the world's best mom is not a dad. That's also why the very best, ideal environment in which a child can be raised is with his or her mother and father.[13] And is it any surprise that "gay and lesbian parents would be more likely to have gay, lesbian, bisexual or unsure (of sexual orientation) sons and daughters"?[14] There *are* ripple effects to our decisions, however well intended those decisions might be.

Sullivan is also quite wrong in thinking that the gay revolution was all about "live and let live." To the contrary, it became clear to me already back in 2004 that for many of the key players who had come out of the closet, their ultimate goal (in fact, it was a necessary goal for their success) was to put conservative Christians (and other conservatives, both religious and nonreligious) in the closet. So I warned in 2011,

> But if cross-dressing and, more radically still, sex-change surgery are fine—after all, we have to be true to ourselves, and, in the end, 'it's my life'—then the day will soon come

when the mutilation of other body parts will be considered fine if it makes the person feel happy and whole. Why not?

Without the male-female order, there would be no human race (it still takes a sperm and an egg to produce a person), and the normalization and celebration of GLBT are a direct assault on the male-female order, leading to gender chaos, to the redefining of marriage, to the remaking of our educational system, to the rewriting of the Bible, to the enshrining of special gay rights even at the expense of religious rights and freedoms of conscience—just to name a few.[15]

The offshoot of all of this is simple. Once you depart from "male and female he created them" (Genesis 1:27)—or simply from biological, functional norms—the course has been set and cannot be stopped. You *will* end up with LGBTQIP+++. You *will* end up with 78 preferred gender pronouns.[16] You *will* end up with "68 Terms That Describe Gender Identity and Expression."[17] You *will* end up with a "Multigender" *Nonbinary Wiki* reference page that lists a number of multigenders, including abigender, ambigender, bigender, demiflux, genderfluid, pangender, polygender, and trigender, all defined with the utmost seriousness.[18] That's why websites devote whole pages to answering questions such as, "What Does the Full LGBTQIA+ Acronym Stand For?"[19] The same website page that answers that question includes a section titled "Understanding LGBTQ2S+ and other expanded acronyms." But of course. Once you deviate from foundational societal norms, the possibilities are endless. That's why the list of preferred gender pronouns has become absolutely (and sadly) laughable, yielding questions like this on the widely visited Quora platform: "Is bun/bunself a valid pronoun? My friend was calling me a transphobe since I said it's not valid."[20]

Add to this the fact that in many schools, from children's schools to universities, students are required to state their PGP's (preferred gender pronouns) at the start of each semester. To fail to do so is to defy your teacher or professor, to be categorized immediately as a bigot, and to be marginalized, often on your first day in school. How is this right, fair, tolerant, or loving? There are even some states and countries that require you to use the preferred name and gender pronoun of a trans-identified co-worker or colleague. To fail to comply will result in stiff fines and potential jail time.

We are *plunging* down that slippery slope! Even when it comes to stating one's personal opposition to same-sex "marriage" based on strongly held religious beliefs, I have colleagues who have lost major business contracts because of their personal beliefs—even though those beliefs never impacted the way they treated others and they had a great track record of working with those who identified as LGBTQ+.

So as much as you care for your cousin Alan, and as much as you have no intention of policing how he and Tim relate romantically or physically, the fact is that once you normalize same-sex relationships, both morally and legally, you set yourself on a dangerous and destructive course. The Lord had reasons for putting certain prohibitions in the Bible, and those reasons were based on His goodness and wisdom, not on some small-minded, bigoted viewpoints.

Unpacking the Point of Law

Let's also consider the question of whether everyone should have the "right" to marry, as long as the people involved are consenting adults. First, why should the number be limited to just two? Or why should it even require two? Are you aware of the rise of sologamy, where people are marrying themselves? (I kid you not. It's a growing industry.) Why should that be wrong?

You might say, "But marriage requires two people!"

I would reply, says who? In fact, the only reason it requires two people is because marriage is the normal way in which a society preserves itself, with men and women joining together to reproduce and care for the next generation. Otherwise, why *can't* you marry yourself? And what do we say to the rising number of polyamorous families in America—allegedly numbering in the hundreds of thousands—along with the increasing acceptance of polygamy?[21] If marriage can be so fundamentally redefined as to include any two people—rather than a man and a woman—why not these other variations?

In reality, there is no valid reason to say "no" to these other unions once you change the very definition of marriage. And that, in fact, is the only reason government gets involved in marriage. As Maggie Gallagher, of the National Organization for Marriage, testified on April 15, 2011, before the United States House of Representatives, Committee on the Judiciary, Subcommittee on the Constitution Hearing on "Defending Marriage,"

Marriage is the union of husband and wife for a reason: these are the only unions that create new life and connect those children in love to their mother and father. . . .

Individuals marry for a hundred private and personal reasons. . . . The public purpose of marriage is the reason why society creates laws around marriage. Here the great public purpose of marriage has always been "responsible procreation"—rooted in the need to protect children by uniting them with the man and woman who made them.

Let's face it: a government license for romantic unions is a strange idea. Adults' intimate relationships, in our legal tradition, are typically nobody else's business. . . .

Why is the government involved in marriage?

The answer in our society, and in virtually every known human society, is that the society recognizes there is an urgent need to bring together men and women to make and raise the next generation together. Marriage is a private desire that serves an urgent public good.

How does marriage protect children? Marriage protects children by increasing the likelihood that children will be born to and raised by their mother and father in one family—and by decreasing the likelihood that the adults will create fatherless children in multiple households. . . .

Marriage is a virtually universal human institution. Every human society has to grapple with three persistent facts about human beings everywhere: sex makes babies, societies need babies, babies deserve a father as well as a mother.[22]

You can hold to these views even if you are not religious. You can certainly hold to these views without bigotry or hatred. What we're talking about is the common good.

It's also fair to ask your cousin Alan and his partner, Tim, how they would feel about two adult gay brothers marrying. After all, the relationship is consensual, not abusive, and there is no possibility of them producing a child with genetic defects, since they cannot reproduce by themselves. (It is well-known that children conceived in incestuous relationships are often born with genetic defects.) Unless Alan and Tim want to invoke the slippery slope argument here, which is something they would otherwise oppose, on what basis should we forbid these gay brothers the right of marriage? After all, love is love, and you have the right to be with the one you love, correct? Haven't we heard that "love wins"?

And what about the phenomenon known as GSA, or genetic sexual attraction? GSA is defined as "sexual attraction between biological relatives who meet for the first time as adults."[23] We are even told that, "Those who claim to have experienced GSA describe it as a very powerful feeling, something they cannot stop or control."[24] What if this applies to these two gay brothers, separated shortly after birth, meeting later in life (both of them turning out to be gay), and now deeply in love? If you say that *they* cannot "marry," but Alan and Tim can, aren't you imposing your own moral or religious values on others? Aren't you guilty of the sin of judging?

I once asked a gay couple this very question. They said to me, "What they do is icky."

I said to them (in a loving and gentle tone), "But you realize that, in my eyes, what you two do is icky. Is that grounds for making it illegal?"

One of them replied, "But you're talking about such a tiny percentage of the population."

To which I responded, "Is it a matter of numbers when it comes to accepting gay relationships? If your numbers were smaller, would that make your argument weaker?"

He agreed that my point was well taken. Yet the same Bible that forbids same-sex relationships also forbids incestuous relationships (see in particular Leviticus 18).

Let's also consider the argument that "I was born this way and cannot change." Does that bring with it a moral imperative? Does that justify our behavior? Every gay man with whom I broached the subject of pedophilia (or pederasty) said that this was wrong—emphatically, unequivocally, and in the strongest possible terms. Wrong, wrong, wrong!

The problem is that adults who are attracted to children will tell you that they, too, feel they were born this way, that they have tried to change, without success, and that the only moral choice they *can* make is to say no to their desires. Many psychologists and psychiatrists would affirm these perceptions, leading to articles with titles like "Sympathy for the Pedophile,"[25] and leading to professionals arguing for the use of new, less stigmatized terms like "minor-attracted persons."[26] (Before "minor-attracted persons," there was "intergenerational intimacy."[27])

To be perfectly clear, I am *not* comparing gays and lesbians engaged in consensual adult relationships to pedophiles or pederasts. No, no, no. But I *am* saying that claiming to be "born that way" proves nothing morally. Or what should we say to those who allegedly have a violent gene or a ruthless gene or an obesity gene?[28] And when it comes to following Jesus, the entry requirement for all is that we *deny ourselves* and take up our cross (see Mark 8:34–36). Plus, there are many ex-gays and ex-lesbians—in fact, their numbers are increasing every year—so we should not rule out the possibility of change. (I should also note that, to this moment, there is no scientific evidence that anyone *is* born gay.)

In short, you can say to Alan, "I love you, and I don't consider myself morally superior to you. And what you do with your life is between you and God. I'm simply saying that my beliefs are grounded in what I understand to be God's best plans for humankind, and when I watch where the push for 'gay rights' has taken our society, I have to say thanks but no thanks. I do not believe this is the best way to go as a nation."

Transgender Activism and Children

When it comes to the subject of transgender identity, we can be even more clear, while expressing tremendous compassion. Who can imagine the torment of feeling as if you have been trapped in the wrong body ever since you were a child? Who can imagine the secrets you had to live with and the sense of freedom you found when you felt harmony between your identity and your gender expression? We can clearly say to someone who identifies as transgender that we do not pretend to understand his or her pain, but that we do care. We don't minimize the person's suffering or mock his or her choices.

At the same time, there is no denying the terribly destructive results of transgender activism. I'm talking about the genital mutilation and chemical castration of children who went through a season of gender confusion, with many of them expressing deep regrets just a few years later. But it's too late to change things now. No wonder some parents are calling this the worst form of medical malpractice we have ever witnessed. Listening to the stories of these young "detransitioners" is truly agonizing. As the famed John Hopkins psychologist Dr. Paul McHugh said to me in a private email dated November 18, 2009, "I hold that interfering medically or surgically with the natural development of young people claiming to be 'transgendered' is a form of child abuse." Precisely so.

The United Kingdom's largest gender clinic, Tavistock Clinic, has now shut down under a growing number of lawsuits, and similar lawsuits are increasing here in America as well.[29] Not surprisingly, other nations, some of them quite "progressive," have now stopped the practice of transitioning children, including Sweden, Norway, and Denmark.[30] And law after law is being passed in the United States to stop biological males from competing in sports competitions with biological females. The push for equal rights for those who identify as transgender has resulted in outright discrimination against women.

That's why lesbian activists like the tennis great Martina Navratilova—along with the famed atheist and biologist Richard Dawkins—along with the bestselling *Harry Potter* author J. K. Rowling (herself a gay and lesbian ally)—along with outspoken atheist and political commentator Bill Maher—along with many other unlikely bedfellows—have also raised their voices in protest against trans activism.[31] All of them see how dangerous the current trajectory is, and all of them realize that reality is not whatever you perceive it to be—unless we want to acknowledge that the hundreds of thousands of people who identify as "furries" are actually part human and part animal.[32] (Did you know that Dr. David Benaron, the inventor who developed the heart monitor technology in our smart watches, identifies as a cheetah named Spottacus?[33])

Psychologists have also pointed to the phenomenon of sociological contagion in conjunction with transgender identity, especially among young people, in particular teenage girls. In an interview on the *Joe Rogan Experience* podcast, psychologist Jordan Peterson made reference to sociological contagion while speaking about these very subjects, noting that "opening the boundaries of 'sex categories' would 'fatally confuse thousands of young girls.'"[34] Peterson also referenced the writings of Henri Ellenberger, in particular his 1970 book *Discovery of the Unconscious*. A new trend takes hold of culture, and suddenly it's as if a significant portion of the society has lost its mind. This helps to explain how the number of kids identifying as trans, especially among girls, has suddenly spiraled out of control.[35]

There is even a new condition known as Rapid Onset Gender Dysphoria (ROGD), and some parents of kids with ROGD had this to say about the contagion:

> Our children are young, naïve and impressionable, many of them are experiencing emotional or social difficulties. They are strongly influenced by their peers and by the media, who are promoting the transgender lifestyle as popular, desirable and the solution to all of their problems. And they are being misled by authority figures, such as teachers, doctors and counselors, who rush to 'affirm' their chosen gender without ever questioning why.[36]

Love compels us to say, "Stop! Surely there is a better way. Surely we must discover how to help these sufferers, both young and old, find healing and wholeness from the inside out."

It's the same with those who suffer from Body Identity Integrity Disorder (BIID, or also BID, for short). These people are so troubled by the presence of healthy limbs or functioning ears or eyes that some of them have successfully amputated limbs or blinded themselves, claiming great peace and satisfaction now that they are handicapped.[37]

Some researchers claim there is a neurological basis for Body Identity Integrity Disorder,[38] just as some researchers claim there is a neurological basis for gender dysphoria, previously called Gender Identity Disorder (GID), before transgender activists successfully had the term *disorder* removed.[39] In the end, though, there is no difference between removing the healthy limb of someone suffering from BIID and removing the healthy breasts of someone suffering from GID. The sufferer might testify to a greatly improved life without breasts or with remodeled private parts, or without hand or foot or arm or leg, or even eyesight. "At last, I feel whole!" they claim.

But those looking on will say, "Surely there must be a better way. Surely we must help these people from the inside out." That's what compassion calls for, especially when we look at the trajectory of where trans activism has already taken us in a few short years.

The good news is that there are more and more ex-trans people as well. Their stories are not just cautionary, as they describe the damage they did to their bodies (and in some cases, to their families and friends). Their stories are

Love compels us to say,
"Stop! Surely there is a better way.
Surely we must discover
how to help these sufferers,
both young and old,
find healing and wholeness
from the inside out."

inspirational as well, as they describe the wonderful new life they enjoy in the Lord. Be encouraged! There is hope.[40]

Mapping Out Your Conversation

Now let's look at a summary of LGBTQ+ issues. On the left in the table that follows, you will find the pro-LGBTQ+ perspective. As I said when we talked about abortion, we need to understand "the other side" if we're to reach out to the *people* who hold such a perspective, while resisting the agenda. On the right in the table you'll find the conservative Christian perspective, which will help you respond both with compassion and a godly, informative reply. Beyond that, to finish our discussion on this issue, you'll find thought-provoking "Questions to Ask" that you can introduce into the discussion when having this difficult, but vitally important, conversation with others.

Summary of Issues

Pro-LGBTQ+ Issue	Response
God made me this way. He is a God of love, and this is the love He has given to me. I cannot change.	God did not design men to be with men and women to be with women. God prohibited homosexual practice because He is good, not bad, because He knows what's best for human flourishing, and because He sees where our decisions and choices ultimately lead.
	Also, other people with less socially accepted attractions (pedophilia or pederasty) also claim to be made that way. Does it make that kind of attraction healthy and morally right?

Pro-LGBTQ+ Issue	Response
I have never been attracted to the opposite sex. Same-sex attraction has always seemed natural to me.	Most people who are same-sex attracted feel this way, as if they were actually born to be gay. But just because something is deeply rooted in our lives and feels natural doesn't mean that it's right. For example, every one of us would say that pedophilia is wrong, yet pedophiles will say that they have always felt that way and it feels natural. Or what about people who have what scientists refer to as an "obesity gene"? Should they celebrate their condition, or should they work harder to overcome obesity, since it is so unhealthy?
I am in a solid, committed same-sex relationship. So are many others I know who are like me.	Would you agree that being in a committed relationship is not the only thing that matters? What if two adult brothers loved each other and wanted to be in a committed, monogamous relationship? Would that make it right? What about gay couples who want to have a child (either by adoption or something like in vitro fertilization)? Is it right for them to deprive the child of either a mother or father by their own choice?
I should be able to marry the person I love. Love is love, and you have the right to be with the one you love.	Once you normalize same-sex relationships, both morally and legally, you set yourself on a dangerous and destructive course. If marriage can be so fundamentally redefined as to include any two people—rather than a man and a woman—why not these other variations, including polyamorous marriages? There is no valid reason to say "no" to such other unions once you change the very definition of marriage. The great public purpose of marriage has always been "responsible procreation"—rooted in the need to protect children by uniting them with the man and woman who conceived them.

Pro-LGBTQ+ Issue	Response
We are good people—we obey the laws, contribute to society, and just want to have our relationship recognized as a marriage.	Once the law rules on a matter (in this case, on the redefining of marriage), then it *does* impact everyone else, like it or not.
LGBTQ+ people are seeking to protect LGBTQ+ identified kids from discrimination or mistreatment and as they attempt to help these kids accept their identities at younger ages.	The results have been disastrous, resulting in massive confusion in the younger generations. There are extensive and costly consequences to this deviation from the basic, male-female ordering of human life and society. Once you deviate from foundational societal norms, the possibilities are endless.
Love is love, no matter what it looks like. You are a bigot if you discriminate the way I want to give and receive sexual love.	When it comes to biological design, it's hard to argue with the fact that men were made for women and women for men—and this is clear for those who believe in evolution, divine creation, or a combination of both. Only males and females can reproduce, only biological men have sperm, only biological women have eggs, and only a biological woman can conceive and nurse a baby. Even in sexual functioning, our bodies are designed to work properly with heterosexual acts more than with homosexual acts. This is biology, not bigotry.

Pro-LGBTQ+ Issue	Response
Children only need a loving home, regardless of whether the home includes parents who are a man and woman, two men, or two women.	Moms and dads are different and unique in ways that are far beyond the uniqueness of two different men or two different women. Research shows clearly that the ideal environment in which a child can be raised is with a mother and a father.
My biological sex does not match who I really am. I have never felt comfortable in my own body, and since becoming trans, I've found new freedom. I would be happy if people would just accept me the way I am.	Is it possible that there are other factors contributing to your gender-identity struggles? What might those be? Sometimes we're looking for solutions in the wrong places. That's why more and more people are "detransitioning" as they discover this—meaning that they seek to go back to their biological sex. It's because hormones and surgery can't fix our deepest internal problems. Also, do you think it's okay for someone who suffers from Body Integrity Identity Disorder (feeling tormented by their healthy limbs or healthy eyes) to amputate their unwanted limbs or blind their seeing eyes? If not, why is it alright to remove or mutilate the healthy organs of someone who identifies as trans?

Questions to Ask

- Do you believe that every kind of expression of love is acceptable?

- Tell me your story. When did you realize that you were _____ (same-sex attracted, transgender, etc.)?

- Tell me your story. When did your _____ (child, sibling, etc.) come out? How has that been for you? How is that relationship today?

- How have you been treated since you came out? Have you been rejected by your family or by the Church?
- If you knew that God did not want you in a same-sex relationship, how would you respond?
- What do you say to those who say they are ex-gay? I want to believe your story, but will you believe *their* story?
- Do you know someone who has gender dysphoria? What have you heard about this serious condition? What have been your observations?
- If you identify as transgender, how long have you felt trapped in the wrong body? Is this something recent, or for as long as you can remember? If you could feel at home in your biological body without any conflict, would you embrace that?

TWELVE

Let's Have a Difficult Conversation

Race Relations

When it comes to Christians and race relationships, many books have been written on this important subject. It's a subject that can divide even devoted Christians. Here, in the space that remains, I want to present food for thought, emphasizing four simple words: *Humility. Sensitivity. Honesty. Commitment.*

Allow me to speak freely as a White, Jewish American. I feel no shame or guilt for being White, nor do I feel any sense of superiority. As to any "privilege" I have, it's common for the majority group in a society to have some kind of privileged status, but in the case of my Jewish family line, that sense of privilege is much less pronounced. My mother was sent to America from England as a little girl.

At a young age, she was abandoned by her father after her mother died, and sent to be raised by relatives here. She didn't have it easy.

My father's parents immigrated from Russia, with my grandfather (whom I never met) dying of lung cancer at the age of forty-four as a result of inhaling fumes as a painter. That left my father, the second of three sons, to become the main breadwinner at the age of eleven. That he worked himself through college and law school, becoming the senior lawyer in the New York Supreme Court, is a testimony to his perseverance and vision, especially when you remember that Jews also faced discrimination in America in centuries past.

Ironically, many Jews fled to America because of serious discrimination and even violent persecution in other parts of the world. Yet you can find examples of overtly antisemitic words, actions, laws, and customs in America from the colonial era down to the present day. These include General Ulysses Grant's expulsion of Jews from areas under his control in Western Tennessee in 1862; the lynching of Leo Frank in 1913; a famous antisemitic manifesto written by car designer Henry Ford in the 1920s; and restrictions on Jewish enrollment in colleges and universities, even in the twentieth century.[1] Today, the highest percentage of religious hate crimes in America are those carried out against Jews.[2] Is this news to you?

Let's Not Ignore Ignorance

Yet whatever previous generations of Jews dealt with here in America, it cannot be compared in the slightest to the suffering and pain endured by Black Americans. Absolutely, categorically not. The suffering of the Jewish people in world history can be compared to the horrors of the slave trade and decades of unequal treatment for African Americans. But not the Jewish American experience alone. Yet truth be told, many White Americans are not fully aware of the scope of Black American suffering, nor do they realize the extent to which the *legacy* of the past remains a current reality for many Black Americans.

Again, I say this without the slightest feeling of "White guilt," or any notion of "White fragility." As I mentioned earlier in the book, my first organ teacher was openly gay (I was just seven at the time). My second organ teacher, however, was a Black man married to a White woman, because of which they had lost family and friends. My father was indignant that such bigoted attitudes could persist in our day (meaning in the early to mid-1960s).

The fact is that many White Americans *are* ignorant of aspects of our nation's past, also failing to recognize how fresh some of the wounds still are and how far we still have to go to achieve our jointly shared vision of equal opportunities (not equal outcomes) for all. I'm reminded of the words of the Catholic scholar Edward Flannery, who, commenting on antisemitism in Church history, wrote,

> The vast majority of Christians, even well educated, are all but totally ignorant of what happened to Jews in history and of the culpable involvement of the Church. . . . It is little exaggeration to state that those pages of history Jews have committed to memory are the very ones that have been torn from Christian (and secular) history books.[3]

The same could be said when it comes to the history of Black Americans. Many White Americans have torn out of their history books the very pages that Black Americans have memorized.

The problem, of course, is that the moment we speak like this, we'll be accused by some of our friends on the right of trying to be "woke," while other friends on the left will accuse us of not going far enough. My advice is not to worry about what people think on either side of the debate. Instead, go to the Lord and say, *Father, I want to please and honor You, and I want to stand for what is important in Your sight. So give me the courage to follow You and Your truth, wherever that may lead.* He will answer sincere prayers like that.

To my White friends, I say this: Let's put down our defenses, let's ignore taunts of "White privilege," and let's not worry about looking "woke." Let's simply ask our friends who are people of color, especially Black Christian friends, to share their perspective with us. Why was the killing of George Floyd so traumatizing to millions of African Americans? Why did most Black observers think O. J. Simpson had been framed by the police, when most White observers thought he was guilty as sin? Why do so many Black Christians in America vote Democrat, despite the party's strong pro-abortion and pro-LGBTQ+ positions? On what basis do many Black Americans (and others) feel that there is still systemic racism here in America?

As for the four words I emphasized at the start, here's their significance:

Humility—We must be willing to learn and to have our blind spots exposed.

Sensitivity—We must take a genuine interest in our neighbor's well-being.

Honesty—We have to embrace the truth, however inconvenient it may be.

Commitment—We have to determine to do what's right if there is something that needs to be fixed.

The Color of Law

Personally, I do not believe that intentional, systemic racism still exists in America. There are Blacks who feel the same. But I understand that there are laws that were birthed out of racism that still remain on our books. Yet I was unaware of this until a Black friend of mine, himself an educator and history professor, pointed me to a book by Richard Rothstein titled *The Color of Law: A Forgotten History of How Our Government Segregated America*.[4] And it is only within the last few years that I learned the history of the Southern Baptists in America, the nation's largest Protestant denomination. As I pointed out in chapter 6, they broke away from the Northern Baptists because they wanted to keep their slaves, and all four founders of the prestigious Southern Baptist Theological Seminary were slaveowners themselves, publicly affirming the Christian right to own slaves.[5] Were you aware of that?

Were you aware that the Louisiana purchase was the result of African slaves fighting for freedom in Haiti?[6] Were you aware that some of the most important inventions of

Black slaves were denied patents? One *Atlanta Black Star* article tells us, "The Patent Act of 1793 and 1836 barred enslaved Africans from obtaining patents because they were not considered citizens."[7] Other such inventions were stolen by the slaves' White owners.[8]

A Black caller to my radio show when I was first on the air was really helpful to me. In my mind, slavery was a thing of the distant past, and segregation a thing of the more recent past. Also, the election of Barack Obama to the presidency demonstrated clearly that we were not the country we used to be. To be sure, there is some truth to this, but the caller helped me realize something else. He rightly noted that Jewish people always point back to the Holocaust, with the motto "Never again!" not far from our lips—especially when Israel is under assault, even though the Holocaust was two generations ago. Segregation in America, however, was much more recent, even though it cannot be compared to the Holocaust itself. More importantly, this caller pointed out, African American history in America, from the days of the colonies until 1964, was always marked by either slavery or segregation in one part of America or another. That helped me realize that it's one thing to forgive the past and move on emotionally, but it's another thing to undo the effects of the past. That would take more time.

And so, while some of us would point to law enforcement statistics indicating that Black suspects are not targeted more by police than White suspects,[9] for many Black Americans, their blatant mistreatment at the hands of the law remains a very real, recent memory. Not only so, but Black Americans tend to think corporately more than their White counterparts do. (Corporate mentality is also commonly found in the Bible, especially in ancient Israelite tribal culture.) So there was the feeling among them that George Floyd was their uncle. A Black pastor once said to me during Obama's presidency, "If you criticize him, just remember that it feels to me as if you're criticizing my son." He wasn't telling me not to say anything; he just wanted me to know how I was being perceived.

I've also had Black Christians call my show, including pastors, and say that they are law abiding, that they live in nice neighborhoods, and that they have never been convicted of a crime—yet when their sons become teenagers, a mom and dad must sit with their young men and urge them to be extremely cautious and respectful when stopped by the police. This is especially true when they have been wrongly stopped because they fit the description of a criminal. One wrong move could cost them their lives.

You might say, "But that's outrageous. They're just being paranoid. The vast majority of cops are good people trying to do a good job."

I would say in response that I certainly hope that the vast majority of cops are good people trying to do a good job, but I don't deny for a moment the experience of my Black friends.

That's also why White and Black reactions were so divided when it came to the O. J. Simpson trial. Most White Americans trusted the law, while many Black Americans did not. The idea that O. J. was being framed seemed preposterous to White observers, but very plausible to Black observers.

After meditating on this for some time, and after extensive, open discussions with my callers over a period of years, walking through difficult situations such as George Zimmerman's killing of Trayvon Martin, I came to this simple conclusion: White Americans often do not see racism when it *is* there. Black Americans often see racism when it is *not* there.

This is why we need to sit and talk and listen to each other, asking for insight and for history. Our minds might not be changed, but at least our perspectives will be broadened. In this context, I think of a call to my show by a Black brother in the immediate aftermath of the death of George Floyd. He said he and his family attended an almost all-White church, but in the midst of the race riots that ensued, the pastor didn't say a single word. The caller wished that, at the least, the pastor had acknowledged that many fellow Americans were in pain right now, including many believers.

I asked this caller, "What would you like me to do?"

He answered, "Just listen. That's all I want. I just want people to know we're hurting."

Again, you might respond, "Hang on for a minute. Forensics indicate that Floyd died of drug abuse, and what the police officer did was standard practice. The officer was wrongly convicted in the court of popular opinion before being unfairly convicted by the courts."

But even if this is true—and it is obviously hotly debated—that does not diminish the perception of our African American brothers and sisters, for whom lynching and systemic police brutality were a way of life not that long ago. To this day, a strong case can be made that, on average, conservative judges give Black criminals longer prison sentences than White criminals who are convicted of similar crimes and who have similar personal backgrounds.[10]

As for the legacy of the past carrying over into this day, a 2021 article in *Business Insider* pointed out that,

> The systemic exclusion of Black Americans from employment, home ownership, and generational wealth is not a new story.
>
> And the wealth gap between Black and White Americans has only persisted: In the fourth quarter of 2020, White households had a total net worth that was over 20 times that of total wealth held by Black households.[11]

This doesn't mean that White Americans should feel guilty or should be obligated by law to share whatever wealth they have. But it does mean that disparities do remain, and that we still have a lot of work to do.

Heading in the Right Direction

Do I believe we are heading in the right direction? Absolutely. Do I believe that the great majority of Americans want to see a level playing field for their fellow citizens? I do. Do I believe that the Diversity, Equity, and Inclusion (DEI) emphasis has done far more harm than good? Without a doubt. Do I believe that groups like BLM have been destructive and that we should wholeheartedly resist Marxism and socialism? Certainly. Do I believe that many of our universities have gone dangerously "woke" and that

Do I believe we are heading
in the right direction?
Absolutely.
Do I believe that the
great majority of Americans
want to see a level playing field
for their fellow citizens?
I do.

the call to be an "antiracist" has all kinds of dangerous overtones? No question.

What I'm advocating for is simply this: Because White Americans have the upper hand historically, socially, and economically to this day, it is important that they sit with their minority colleagues—especially fellow brothers and sisters in the Lord, be they Black or Hispanic or Asian or Native American—and say, "Please share your perspective with me on what's happening today in the news regarding racism. Please explain why you vote the way you do."

Then, once you have demonstrated that you really want to listen and learn, you will likely be invited to share your perspective as well. (I've focused here on Black-White relations, but obviously, there's a massive discussion to have with our Native American friends, as well as with other minorities.) In this context, I remember a Black pastor in New York City saying to me, "You want to get prayer back in the schools. I want to get education back in the schools." How different were our starting points!

Mapping Out Your Conversation

Now let's look at a summary of race relations issues. On the left in the table that follows, you'll find the Black American perspective, as I understand it from my conversations with Black American friends and colleagues, and as best I can express it—in overly generalized terms, obviously, since there is great diversity in the Black American community. (If you live outside the United States, by the way, undoubtedly your country also faces race relations issues. Please translate what I'm sharing here into your context.) Note that there isn't so much an agenda to resist with this issue, as *there is a middle ground to discover*. So on the right, you'll find what might be called a "standard" White American perspective—again, in overly generalized terms. Comparing the two sides of the table will help you see the differences in viewpoint between the races and explore in conversations with others what could become a more balanced perspective on both sides. (Such a table could be made for the interchange between any two races in any country, but here I've focused on the Black and the White in America since that was my specific focus in this chapter.) Beyond the table, to finish our discussion on this issue, you'll find thought-provoking "Questions to Ask" that you can introduce into the discussion when you are having this difficult, but vitally important, conversation with others.

Summary of Issues

Black Perspective	White Perspective
America has deeply racist roots, and despite all the progress that has been made since our founding, systemic racism still exists in our country.	America is a wonderful country with strong Judeo-Christian roots, although slavery and segregation were terrible sins that marred our history. But those past sins don't define us, nor is racism present in any systemic way in our society today.

Black Perspective	White Perspective
As the dominant, founding, and ruling majority, White Americans still have clear advantages (i.e., privilege) over Black Americans, right up until this day. Just consider the disparity in net worth between the average Black family and average White family.	The election of Barak Obama to the presidency, coupled with the tremendous success of Black Americans in the worlds of business, education, media, entertainment, and sports, indicates that the playing field has been leveled and our country really is the land of endless opportunity for all.
To this day, Black Americans are subject to more police brutality and racial profiling than White Americans. Need we say more than *George Floyd*? On average, Blacks are also sentenced to longer prison sentences than Whites for committing the same crimes.	While the death of George Floyd was tragic, there's no evidence that it was race related. Some studies indicate that his death was drug related. Statistics also demonstrate that Black policemen are more likely to shoot a Black suspect than are White policemen. Studies claiming racism in the courts have also been brought into question.
Whites have no idea what it's like to be a Black American. There are additional obstacles facing Blacks at every turn, from job opportunities to being stereotyped and categorized. Black businessmen flying first class even get odd looks, as if the only successful Blacks are expected to be either athletes or rappers.	Many Blacks think that their communities are believing lies and are perceiving racism when it's not even there. Not only so, but affirmative action has actually resulted in reverse discrimination, withholding opportunities from highly qualified Whites.

Black Perspective	White Perspective
While groups like BLM may have gone to extremes, they became so powerful so quickly because they tapped into the very real past-and-present pain of Black Americans.	Groups like BLM are part of a dangerous agenda to turn America into a Marxist country where people are divided into the oppressors and the oppressed. They do far more harm than good.

Questions to Ask

- Please share your perspective with me on what's happening today in the news regarding racism.
- Please share with me why you vote the way you do.
- What is your experience when it comes to the question of police brutality against minorities, or systemic injustice? What do you feel is real, and what is imagined?
- What are your thoughts about groups like BLM and Antifa? Are they following in the footsteps of the Civil Rights movement, or do you think they have hijacked a powerful movement for their own purposes?
- Tell me what blind spots you think I might have. And, if you can, tell me where you might have some blind spots.
- Do you agree with the following statement? "The White majority often doesn't see racism when it is there, and people of color in the minority often see racism when it is not there."

- What do you appreciate about this country, both in the past and in the present? What aspects of this country's past or present grieve you?
- How is biblical justice the same or different than what today is called "social justice"?
- It's not possible (or even healthy) to try to achieve equal outcomes for all, but what do you think still needs to be done to achieve equal opportunities for all, as much as is humanly possible?

CONCLUSION

An Unstoppable Formula

In the previous chapter, I emphasized four simple words that are vital keys to reaching out with courage and compassion to people who have different perspectives than we do, even as we resist their damaging agendas. Those four words are *humility, sensitivity, honesty*, and *commitment*. Once we have learned to listen to each other with humility and sensitivity, to be honest with one another, and to commit to honor and respect one another rather than arguing, then we can bow before God as one, looking at the high standards of the Word and its constant calls for justice and mercy, working together to make our nation better for all.

In this way, too, we can demonstrate to the world that we are disciples of Jesus, loving one another, loving our neighbors, and letting our light shine brightly with hearts of compassion and backbones of steel. It is an unstoppable formula.

We can demonstrate to the world
that we are disciples of Jesus,
loving one another,
loving our neighbors,
and letting our light shine brightly
with hearts of compassion
and backbones of steel.
It is an unstoppable formula.

Shall we join together, then, as children of God, as lovers of His Word, as people of conviction filled with love and with truth, and bring a smile to the Father's face? Shall we join together to preach the Good News to the poor and to set the captives free?

It's true that we live in very difficult and contentious times, times that strain the very fabric of the nation. It's true that the divisions are very deep, threatening to tear us apart. But this only means that it's time for the Church of Jesus to sparkle like never before. Let's arise and shine!

HELPFUL RESOURCES

Below is a short list of recommended resources that will help you learn more about the issues discussed in this book. I have also put together a more extensive list of websites, articles, videos, and books on my website at TheLineOf Fire.org/RecommendedResources.

Other Books by Michael L. Brown

- *Can You Be Gay and Christian?* This book provides a solid biblical answer to this question and explains how you can respond with love and truth when having conversations about homosexuality with others.
- *A Queer Thing Happened to America.* This book chronicles the shocking transformation of America over the last forty years.
- *The Silencing of the Lambs.* This book explores the rise of cancel culture and how Christians can stand in faith and overcome it.
- *Turn the Tide.* This book provides the information you need to be used by the Holy Spirit to

bring reformation to our society in the wake of spiritual revival, including how to be grounded in apologetics and engage the culture wars in the power of the Spirit.

Websites

- Apologetics315.com. This website provides educational resources for the defense of the Christian faith, with the goal of strengthening the faith of believers and engaging the questions and challenges of other world views.
- CARM.org. This website from Christian Apologetics and Resource Ministries has many articles on the topics of chapters 10–12. Simply type the topic in their search box.

Videos

At TheLineOfFire.org/RecommendedResources you will find several links to videos on these topics:

- What does the Bible say about homosexuality?
- Is homosexuality consistent with New Testament obedience?
- In His image
- Tranzformed—finding peace with your God-given gender
- What the Bible says about sexuality
- How to respond to LGBT dilemmas

Articles

- You can read articles on the topics in this book and many others at TheLineOfFire.org/Articles/Topic. See specifically the following:
  - TheLineOfFire.org/Articles/Topic/Race-Relations
  - TheLineOfFire.org/Articles/Topic/LGBTQ
  - TheLineOfFire.org/Articles/Topic/Abortion
- Search thousands of topics on CARM.org.

NOTES

Chapter 1 "They Sound Just Like Us"

1. Alex Nguyen and William Melhado, "Gov. Greg Abbott signs legislation barring trans youth from accessing trans-related care," the *Texas Tribune*, June 2, 2023 (updated June 3), https://www.texastribune.org/2023/06/02/texas-gender-affirming-care-ban/.

2. See Lawrence B. Finer, Lori F. Frohwirth, Lindsay A. Dauphinee, Susheela Singh, and Ann M. Moore, "Reasons U.S. Women Have Abortions: Quantitative and Qualitative Perspectives," Guttmacher Institute, https://www.guttmacher.org/sites/default/files/pdfs/pubs/psrh/full/3711005.pdf. (Note that this is from a pro-choice study, not a pro-life study.)

Chapter 2 Recognize That We All Have Blind Spots

1. John Newton, "Amazing Grace," written 1772 and published 1779, public domain.

2. John Newton, *Thoughts Upon the African Slave Trade* (London: J. Buckland and J. Johnson, 1788), found online at https://en.wikisource.org/wiki/Thoughts_upon_the_African_Slave_Trade.

3. See "John Newton's Letter on His Conversion," *Baby Blue Online* (blog), November 29, 2006, https://babybluecafe.blogspot.com/2006/11/john-newtons-letter-on-his-conversion.html.

4. John Newton, *Thoughts Upon the African Slave Trade*, https://en.wikisource.org/wiki/Thoughts_upon_the_African_Slave_Trade.

5. John Newton, *Letters to a Wife: By the Author of Cardiphonia* (London: J. Johnson, 1793), cited in Marylynn Rouse, John Newton (1725–1807), contributed to Brycchan Carey online at https://brycchancarey.com/abolition/newton.htm.

6. "John Newton: Reformed slave trader," *Christianity Today* Christian History pages online, https://www.christianitytoday.com/history/people/pastorsandpreachers/john-newton.html.

7. I want to note that for a long time I have advocated changing the name of the book of *James* to the book of *Jacob*. To explain why would be too far off topic in this particular book, but suffice to say that there are many solid linguistic and historical reasons to do so. For more information and insight on this, see my *The Line of Fire* article of March 11, 2013, "Recovering the Lost Letter of Jacob," found at https://thelineoffire.org/article/recovering-the-lost-letter-of-jacob.

Chapter 3 "Reach Out and Resist"

1. Dr. R. Albert Mohler Jr., "There Is No 'Third Way'—Southern Baptists Face a Moment of Decision (and so will you)," Albert Mohler online, June 2, 2014, https://albertmohler.com/2014/06/02/there-is-no-third-way-southern-baptists-face-a-moment-of-decision-and-so-will-you.

2. Soulforce, "Our History," https://soulforce.org/about/our-history/.

3. Not all of the letters were in place then, but most of the concepts were.

Chapter 4 Even When Total Honesty Hurts, Love Tells the Truth

1. Paul Bois, "Meet Ooti, The Uterus: An Emoji For Planned Parenthood," *Daily Wire*, August 21, 2017, https://www.dailywire.com/news/so-thing-now-uterus-emojis-planned-parenthood-paul-bois.

2. You can listen to this entire call (or read the transcript) on *The Line of Fire* episode "Christian Working at Planned Parenthood Vows Never to Return: 'It's Not Tissue! They Are Babies!,'" YouTube video, run time 18:26, July 29, 2017, https://www.youtube.com/watch?v=BSmnPhAWU0c.

3. Guest Column, "Planned Parenthood staffer quits after seeing aborted children: 'It's murder,'" *Live Action News*, September 6, 2017, https://www.liveaction.org/news/former-planned-parenthood-see-baby-sucking-thumb/.

4. Ibid. See also the *Live Action News* three-part series of articles found at https://www.liveaction.org/news/planned-parenthood-manager-grief-journals/.

5. "Thomas Sowell > Quotes," Goodreads, Inc., https://www.goodreads.com/author/quotes/2056.Thomas_Sowell.

6. I found this Jean Daillé quote many years ago in a book of quotes, without original attribution. I no longer have that book available to cite, but an Internet search confirms the wording at several sources.

7. For more on this, see my article "A Plea for Ministerial Clarity," *The Line of Fire*, February 3, 2023, https://thelineoffire.org/article/a-plea-for-ministerial-clarity. Also, for many more resources that will help you make your own voice heard for moral sanity and spiritual clarity, visit https://thelineoffire.org.

Chapter 5 "Overcome Evil with Good"

1. Dr. Michael Brown, "The Gay Protest That Encountered the Love of God," *The Line of Fire*, August 28, 2012, https://thelineoffire.org/article/the-gay-protest-that-encountered-the-love-of-god.

2. Dr. Michael Brown, "FIRE Church Welcomes Charlotte's LGBT Community," *In the Line of Fire* (blog), August 25, 2012, http://lineoffireblog.blogspot.com/2012/08/fire-church-welcomes-charlottes-lgbt.html.

3. Brown, "The Gay Protest," https://thelineoffire.org/article/the-gay-protest-that-encountered-the-love-of-god.

4. Ibid.

5. Ibid.

6. Ibid.

7. For more on how this scenario played out, you can listen to *The Line of Fire* radio broadcast episode "Update on the Gay Protest at FIRE Church, Dr. Brown Reflects on God's Grace and Answers Your Questions," August 27, 2012, https://lineoffireradio.com/2012/08/27/update-on-the-gay-protest-at-fire-church-dr-brown-reflects-on-gods-grace-and-answers-your-questions/.

8. The protest leader never followed through on my request to arrange for me to meet with local professing gay Christians, not so I could debate them, but so they could share their stories and tell me how they viewed people like me. Perhaps, only knowing me from a distance, these others were not about to sit face-to-face with me. Or perhaps they had been hurt too much to open their hearts again to someone like me.

9. If you'd like to read the article yourself, you can find it in my ASKDrBrown archives at https://archive.askdrbrown.org/library/misrepresent-and-demonize-weapon-%E2%80%98progressive%E2%80%99-christians.

10. Dr. Michael Brown, "Misrepresent and Demonize: The Weapon of 'Progressive' Christians," ASKDrBrown, May 23, 2019, https://archive.askdrbrown.org/library/misrepresent-and-demonize-weapon-%E2%80%98progressive%E2%80%99-christians. (Also see my original article, "It's Time for California Parents to Defy the Law," which I had linked to the quoted article. You can find it in the ASKDrBrown archives at https://archive.askdrbrown.org/library/it's-time-california-parents-defy-law.)

11. Ibid.

12. For more of Sarahbeth's story, see "From Deconstruction to Reconstruction: a story of doubt to faith," Sarahbeth Caplin online, April 22, 2022, https://sbethcaplin.com/2022/04/22/from-deconstruction-to-reconstruction-a-story-of-doubt-to-faith/.

13. Dr. Michael Brown's Facebook page, August 19, 2023, https://www.facebook.com/ASKDrBrown/posts/pfbid02DibaHeJG34FqEa9D7ymEuxmm9pi8cfpb3AaSfgiUKKf5PhHy9k33t4VfrQpeLN3tl.

Chapter 6 Enrolling in Shared Humanity 101

1. For more about my mother, see the memorial I wrote about her on the day she died, "In Memory of My Mom, Rose G. Brown," which you can find in my ASKDrBrown archives at https://archive.askdrbrown.org/library/memory-my-mom-rose-g-brown-sept-25-1922-nov-18-2016.

2. For more on this, see R. Albert Mohler Jr., with collaborators Dr. Curtis Woods, Dr. John Wilsey, Dr. Kevin Jones, Dr. Jarvis Williams, Dr. Matthew

J. Hall, and Dr. Gregory Wills, "Report in Slavery and Racism in the History of the Southern Baptist Theological Seminary," Southern Baptist Theological Seminary, December 12, 2018, https://www.sbts.edu/history/southern-project/.

Chapter 7 Hijacked by Demonic Forces

1. For more on this, see *Wikipedia*, s.v. "Women's International Terrorist Conspiracy from Hell," last edited January 17, 2024, https://en.wikipedia.org/wiki/Women%27s_International_Terrorist_Conspiracy_from_Hell.

2. This is my paraphrase of some of their sentiments, not an actual quote. For these pro-abortion accounts firsthand, see Amelia Bonow and Emily Nokes, eds., *Shout Your Abortion* (Oakland, Cali.: PM Press, 2018).

3. Patrick Reilly, "USA Powerlifting to allow trans athletes to compete with women after losing suit," *New York Post* online, March 4, 2023, https://nypost.com/2023/03/04/usa-powerlifting-to-allow-trans-athletes-to-compete-after-losing-suit/.

4. Dr. R. Albert Mohler Jr., "Moralistic Therapeutic Deism—the New American Religion," Albert Mohler online, April 11, 2005, https://albertmohler.com/2005/04/11/moralistic-therapeutic-deism-the-new-american-religion-2.

5. Carver Fisher, "Logan Paul gets shredded by fans after attacking best friend's religion," Dexerto, December 17, 2022, https://www.dexerto.com/entertainment/logan-paul-gets-shredded-by-fans-after-attacking-best-friends-religion-2013640/.

6. See also the chapter "If Gay Is Good, the Church is Bad" in my book *Why So Many Christians Have Left the Faith*.

7. Perry L. Glanzer, "Is Empathy a Christian Virtue? Comparing Empathy to Christian Compassion," *Christian Scholar's Review*, June 13, 2022, https://christianscholars.com/is-empathy-a-christian-virtue-comparing-empathy-to-christian-compassion-2/.

8. Ayn Rand, *The Romantic Manifesto: A Philosophy of Literature* (New York: New American Library, 1975, 1971), 131.

9. See also the final chapter in John L. Cooper's book *Wimpy, Weak, and Woke: How Truth Can Save America from Utopian Destruction*, where he points to the implications of a real Kingdom vision. (Cooper is lead vocalist, bassist, and songwriter/producer for Skillet.)

10. To watch this yourself, see "Tyra part 5 Transgender children and their parents speak out," YouTube video, run time 6:15, posted by gik70, March 2, 2010, https://www.youtube.com/watch?v=E1o2Im6t6Mo.

Chapter 9 "The Lord's Servant Must Not Be Quarrelsome"

1. George W. Knight III, *The Pastoral Epistles: A Commentary on the Greek Text*, part of *The New International Greek Testament Commentary*, eds. I. Howard Marshall and W. Ward Gasque (Grand Rapids: W. B. Eerdmans; Carlisle, England: Paternoster Press, 1992), 423.

2. Matthew Henry, *Matthew Henry's Commentary on the Whole Bible: Complete and Unabridged in One Volume* (Peabody, Mass.: Hendrickson, 1994), 2363.

Chapter 10 Let's Have a Difficult Conversation: Abortion

1. For more on the challenges of responding to such a scenario as believers, see Penny Young Nance, "A Sensitive Response to Rape," *Christian Post*, November 2, 2012, https://www.christianpost.com/news/a-sensitive-response-to-rape.html.

2. Nance, "A Sensitive Response to Rape," https://www.christianpost.com/news/a-sensitive-response-to-rape.html.

3. Ibid.

4. Ibid.

5. "Catherine" (the name in the article was changed to protect her identity), BBC, November 22, 2017, https://www.bbc.com/news/stories-42055511.

6. For more on Jude's story and for the latest update, visit the "Praying for Jude Sullivan Peters" Facebook page, found at https://www.facebook.com/prayingforjudesullivanpeters.

7. Julian Quinones and Arijeta Lajka, "What kind of society do you want to live in?" Inside the country where Down syndrome is disappearing," *CBSN: On Assignment*, updated August 15, 2017, https://www.cbsnews.com/news/down-syndrome-iceland/.

8. HealthyWomen Editors, "Families With a Child With Down Syndrome Say Experiences Are Positive," HealthyWomen, March 22, 2016, https://www.healthywomen.org/content/article/families-child-down-syndrome-say-experiences-are-positive.

9. Jeanne Mancini, "People with Down syndrome are happy. Why are we trying to eliminate them?", *Washington Post*, August 24, 2017, https://www.washingtonpost.com/news/posteverything/wp/2017/08/24/people-with-down-syndrome-are-happy-why-are-we-trying-to-eliminate-them/.

Chapter 11 Let's Have a Difficult Conversation: LGBTQ+

1. Andrew Sullivan, "The Queers Versus The Homosexuals," *Weekly Dish*, May 19, 2023, https://andrewsullivan.substack.com/p/the-queers-versus-the-homosexuals-cfd.

2. Ibid.

3. Ibid.

4. Ibid.

5. "Libraries Respond: Drag Queen Story Hour," American Library Association (ALA), https://www.ala.org/advocacy/libraries-respond-drag-queen-story-hour.

6. For more on this, see Michael L. Brown, *A Queer Thing Happened to America: And What a Long, Strange Trip It's Been* (Concord, N.C.: EqualTime Books, 2011), 84–119.

7. For more on this, see again *A Queer Thing Happened to America*, 84–119, and also 120–150. Likewise, visit my online Opinion article "Sociological Contagion and the Growing Non-Binary Movement," *Daily Wire*, https://www.dailywire.com/news/sociological-contagion-and-the-growing-non-binary-movement.

8. From the back cover of the 2002 edition of *GENDERqueer*, Riki Wilchins, Clare Howe, and Joan Nestle, eds. (Los Angeles: Alyson Books, 2002).

9. Patrick Califia-Rice, "Two Dads with a Difference—Neither of Us Was Born Male," *Village Voice*, June 21–27, 2000.

10. Brown, *A Queer Thing*, 551–52.

11. Ibid., 551.

12. Ibid., 552.

13. For more on this, see for example Jeff Johnston, "Kids Need a Mom and a Dad—That's What the Research Shows," *Daily Citizen*, February 26, 2018, https://dailycitizen.focusonthefamily.com/kids-need-a-mom-and-a-dad-thats-what-the-research-shows/.

14. Walter R. Schumm, "Children of Homosexuals More Apt to Be Homosexuals? A Reply to Morrison and to Cameron Based on an Examination of Multiple Sources of Data," published online by Cambridge University Press from the *Journal of Biosocial Science*, July 20, 2010, https://www.cambridge.org/core/journals/journal-of-biosocial-science/article/abs/children-of-homosexuals-more-apt-to-be-homosexuals-a-reply-to-morrison-and-to-cameron-based-on-an-examination-of-multiple-sources-of-data/A9A564AF4D13FC42A78E67868C590FD4.

15. Brown, *A Queer Thing*, 596–97.

16. For more detail, see the article "What are the 78 Gender pronouns?," *Bob Cut Mag*, September 7, 2021, https://bobcutmag.com/2021/09/07/what-are-the-78-gender-pronouns/.

17. Mere Abrams and Sian Ferguson, "68 Terms That Describe Gender Identity and Expression," healthline, last reviewed February 9, 2022, https://www.healthline.com/health/different-genders.

18. For more detail, see *Nonbinary Wiki*, s.v. "Multigender," last edited July 17, 2023, https://nonbinary.wiki/wiki/Multigender.

19. For more detail, see Kevin Le, "What Does the Full LGBTQIA+ Acronym Stand For?," GoodRX Health, last updated October 19, 2022, https://www.goodrx.com/health-topic/lgbtq/meaning-of-lgbtqia.

20. For more detail, see https://www.quora.com/Is-bun-bunself-a-valid-pronoun-My-friend-was-calling-me-a-transphobe-since-I-said-its-not-valid.

21. Frank Newport, "Understanding the Increase in Moral Acceptability of Polygamy," Gallup.com: Polling Matters, June 26, 2020, https://news.gallup.com/opinion/polling-matters/313112/understanding-increase-moral-acceptability-polygamy.aspx.

22. United States House of Representatives Committee on the Judiciary, Subcommittee on the Constitution Hearing on "Defending Marriage," April 15, 2011, Statement of Maggie Gallagher, National Organization for

Marriage, https://judiciary.house.gov/sites/evo-subsites/judiciary.house.gov /files/2016-04/Gallagher04152011.pdf.

23. "Incest," GoodTherapy.org, last updated May 8, 2018, https://www .goodtherapy.org/blog/psychpedia/incest#:~:text=Genetic%20sexual%20attrac tion%20%28GSA%29%20is%20a%20term%20used,or%20half-siblings%20 meet%20in%20adulthood%2C%20or%20between%20cousins.

24. Ibid.

25. Found at https://quillandquire.com/authors/2007/03/05/sympathy-for -the-pedophile/.

26. Found at https://www.mdedge.com/psychiatry/article/242357/minor -attracted-persons-neglected-population.

27. For more on this, see https://www.christianpost.com/voices/from-in tergenerational-intimacy-to-minor-attracted-persons.html.

28. For more on this, see Brown, *A Queer Thing*, 213–15.

29. For more on this, see Libby Brooks, "Tavistock gender identity clinic is closing: what happens next?," *Guardian*, last amended August 3, 2022, https:// www.theguardian.com/society/2022/jul/28/tavistock-gender-identity-clinic-is -closing-what-happens-next. See also Merrill Matthews, "Matthews: Here come the gender-detransition lawsuits," The Hill, October 31, 2023, https:// thehill.com/opinion/4284777-matthews-here-come-the-gender-detransitioner -lawsuits/.

30. For more on this, see my Analysis article "While Other Countries Hit The Brakes On Transitioning Children, America Is Hitting The Gas," *Daily Wire*, https://www.dailywire.com/news/while-other-countries-hit-the-brakes -on-transitioning-children-america-is-hitting-the-gas.

31. For more on this, see my article "Woke Won't Work," *The Line of Fire*, January 15, 2024, https://thelineoffire.org/article/woke-wont-work.

32. For a pro-furry perspective, see Sharon E. Roberts, "What are 'fur- ries?' Debunking myths about kids identifying as animals, and litter boxes in schools," *The Conversation*, November 7, 2022, https://theconversation .com/what-are-furries-debunking-myths-about-kids-identifying-as-animals -and-litter-boxes-in-schools-193908.

33. For more on this, see Will Greenwald, "Your Smartwatch's Heart Rate Monitor Was Developed by a Furry," *PCMag*, June 4, 2022, https:// www.pcmag.com/news/your-smartwatchs-heart-rate-monitor-was-developed -by-a-furry.

34. Hannah Sparks, "Jordan Peterson on Joe Rogan Show: Being trans is like 'satanic ritual abuse,'" *New York Post*, January 27, 2022, https://ny post.com/2022/01/27/joe-rogan-guest-jordan-peterson-says-being-trans-is -a-contagion/.

35. For more on this, see Henri F. Ellenberger, *The Discovery of the Un- conscious: The History and Evolution of Dynamic Psychiatry* (New York: Basic Books, 1981).

36. "Who We Are," Rapid-Onset Gender Dysphoria (ROGD), https:// www.parentsofrogdkids.com.

37. For the story of Jewel Shuping, who blinded herself, see my article "Lessons from the woman who blinded herself," *WND*, October 27, 2015, http://www.wnd.com/2015/10/lessons-from-the-woman-who-blinded -herself/.

38. For one example of this, visit http://journals.plos.org/plosone/article ?id=10.1371/journal.pone.0072212.

39. For one example of this, visit http://www.scientificamerican.com /article/is-there-something-unique-about-the-transgender-brain/.

40. For some of these people's stories, see the powerful documentary "In His Image: Delighting in God's Plan for Gender and Sexuality," YouTube video, run time 1:43:42, posted by In His Image Movie, March 12, 2021, https://www.youtube.com/watch?v=W3YKpnrzmqc. See also Walt Heyer's book *Trans Life Survivors* (Chatham, N.J.: Bowker, 2018).

Chapter 12 Let's Have a Difficult Conversation: Race Relations

1. For more on this, see *Wikipedia*'s "History of antisemitism in the United States," https://en.wikipedia.org/wiki/History_of_antisemitism_in _the_United_States. A *Washington Post* article online also tells us that elite universities restricted Jewish enrollment a century ago. They created the modern college admissions process. (You can find the article at https://www.wash ingtonpost.com/education/2023/11/13/how-restricting-jews-created-modern -college-admissions/.)

2. Ron Kampeas, "Jews again faced the most hate crimes of any religious group in 2022, FBI reports," Jewish Telegraphic Agency (JTA), October 17, 2023, https://www.jta.org/2023/10/17/united-states/jews-again-faced-the -most-hate-crimes-of-any-religious-group-in-2022-fbi-reports.

3. Edward H. Flannery, *The Anguish of the Jews: Twenty-Three Centuries of Antisemitism* (New York/Mahwah: Paulist Press, 1985), 1.

4. Richard Rothstein, *The Color of Law: A Forgotten History of How Our Government Segregated America* (New York: Liveright, 2017).

5. For more on this, see R. Albert Mohler Jr., with collaborators Dr. Curtis Woods, Dr. John Wilsey, Dr. Kevin Jones, Dr. Jarvis Williams, Dr. Matthew J. Hall, and Dr. Gregory Wills, "Report in Slavery and Racism in the History of the Southern Baptist Theological Seminary," Southern Baptist Theological Seminary, December 12, 2018, https://www.sbts.edu/history /southern-project/.

6. For more on this, see the History.com article "The Louisiana Purchase Was Driven by a Slave Rebellion," https://www.history.com/news/louisiana -purchase-price-french-colonial-slave-rebellion.

7. Tracy, "5 Inventions By Enslaved Black Men Blocked By U.S. Patent Office," *Atlanta Black Star*, last updated February 16, 2019, https://atlan-tablackstar.com/2014/02/11/5-inventions-by-enslaved-black-men-blocked-by -us-patent-office/.

8. "America's always had black inventors—even when the patent system explicitly excluded them," *The Conversation*, February 14, 2017, https://

theconversation.com/americas-always-had-black-inventors-even-when-the-patent-system-explicitly-excluded-them-72619.

9. For more on this, see Heather Mac Donald, *The War on Cops: How the New Attack on Law and Order Makes Everyone Less Safe* (New York: Encounter Books, 2016).

10. For more on this, see Radley Balko, "There's overwhelming evidence that the criminal justice system is racist. Here's the proof," *Washington Post*, June 10, 2020, https://www.washingtonpost.com/graphics/2020/opinions/systemic-racism-police-evidence-criminal-justice-system/. See also Edwin Rios, "Racial inequality over long US prison sentences growing, report finds," *Guardian*, July 21, 2022, https://www.theguardian.com/us-news/2022/jul/21/prisons-us-racial-equality-black-white-americans.

11. Juliana Kaplan and Madison Hoff, "These 2 charts show how the racial wealth gap has gotten even wider over the years," *Business Insider*, March 24, 2021, https://www.businessinsider.com/charts-how-much-wealth-each-race-ethnicity-held-2020-2021-3.

MICHAEL L. BROWN, Ph.D. (New York University), hosts the nationally syndicated daily talk radio show and podcast *The Line of Fire* and is Director of Spiritual Renewal and Apologetics at the Jerusalem Bible Institute. He has served as a visiting or adjunct professor at eight seminaries and is widely considered to be the world's  foremost Messianic Jewish apologist. He has preached throughout America and around the world, bringing a message of repentance, revival, and cultural reformation.

Dr. Brown has written more than 45 books, including *Has God Failed You?*, *Not Afraid of the Antichrist*, *60 Questions Christians Ask About Jewish Beliefs and Practices*, and the *Answering Jewish Objections to Jesus* series. He comments that "I wake up every day with a heart burning to change the world. To see the Church ablaze. To see my Jewish people come to faith."

He and his wife Nancy, who is also a Jewish believer in Jesus, have been married since 1976. They have two daughters and four grandchildren. To learn more about Dr. Brown and his ministry, visit www.thelineoffire.org.